EXCERPTS FROM THE THIRD TESTAMENT

Copyright © translation by Darin Stoytchev
Editors: Lynn Sirove & Hal Lingerman

This book is available in digital format for free together with the books "Love Wisdom Truth," "The Might of Love" and "Prayers and Spiritual Formulas;" send an email to: mainpem@gmail.com.

Published in Santa Monica, CA U.S.A
Copyright © 2019 All rights reserved.

The Master Beinsa Duno/Peter Dunov

Foreword

Beinsa Duno/Peter Dunov is a spiritual Master who was born on 07/11/1864 in the village of Nikolaevka, Varna district, Bulgaria, and departed on 12/27/1944 Sofia, Bulgaria.

Jesus Christ gave us precious Divine knowledge, but we need to add to that knowledge; we need to expand our understanding of His teachings and to apply them in our lives. Beinsa Duno, I believe, is one of the best sources to help us understand and expand the Divine teachings Christ gave us. The essence of the Teaching of Beinsa Duno is the love of God, brotherhood and sisterhood among all people, the love of all living beings and the love of all plants. My intention of this collection of thoughts and translation is to help those who want spiritual development and progress. Just as good physical food is important for our body to function well, so is good spiritual food important for our spiritual lives.
About the translation: I did my best together with the help of the editors Lynn Sirove and Hal Lingerman to translate the spirit of the thoughts the Master gave. As you are likely aware, no matter how good a translation is, there is always something that gets lost even in the best translation. In some places you will find sentences that do not appear to be English, I believe had I made them sound better the meaning of the thought or the style of expression would have changed. I would like also to mention that according to some Bulgarian language literature specialists, some of Beinsa Duno's grammar and/or literature expressions (in Bulgarian language) they did not consider correct as well. The order in

which the words are put in a sentence and their sounds produce certain vibrations and certain results in us. The literature specialists maybe right from their point of view, they follow certain grammar and/or literature man-made rules. However we should keep in mind that Masters are conductors of the Divine and whatever they say supersedes anything said by humans. In the book I have decided to keep with the gender style of expression used in the spiritual books. Within a given writing where "man" is used the reader will need to comprehend on his own when it is used a general comment and does not imply a specific gender or when it is used specifically to denote a specific gender. In one and the same lecture oftentimes one brother or sister understands the thoughts in one way or another in a different way; but both of them could well be right for themselves because they understood the thoughts according to their level of their development. Beinsa Duno says the Scriptures are written in three languages. The language of the ordinary people, the talented and the genius. We all are on a different level of development. I think it is still better to read something than nothing; follow your intuition and instincts for a better understanding the meaning of the thoughts.

Somewhere you may read that Beinsa Duno preached a form of Esoteric Christianity or that he was a sect leader. After studying the lectures of the Master for over 25 years, I deem both definitions wrongful.

Lastly about the title of the book. Why did I use this title for the book? I remember reading in a lecture in which Beinsa Duno asked the question: "Where does it say in the Bible that there will not be a Third Testament?" In my view and according also to some other followers of Jesus Christ and Beinsa Duno, the lectures Beinsa Duno gave are the Third Testament. They are the continuation of the Bible. This book is comprised of excerpts from the Third Testament and thus I came up with the idea for the name.

(This book is available in digital format for free together with the books "Love Wisdom Truth", "The Might of Love" and "Prayers and Spiritual Formulas"; send an email to: mainpem@gmail.com.)

Enjoy your reading!
Peace, Love, and Light. God be with you.
Darin Stoytchev

EXCERPTS FROM THE THIRD TESTAMENT

The whole world is designed to learn three things: **to learn what Love is, to learn what Wisdom is, to learn what God's Truth is.** Then learn the life that flows out of Love and what it should be like. To learn the light, that flows from the Divine Wisdom, what it must be and the freedom which flows out from the Truth, what it must be; this you will study here on Earth and up in heaven, wherever you may be, even if you are in Hell you will study these things. However, if you are in hell, the methods are different. There, the teachers carry big sticks and when you do not know, they give you a beating. In Paradise are the best teachers; there is no punishment there, the students are diligent, they do not shirk duty and they are ideal students. Each student learns his lesson well. In Hell they shirk, go around, just like here, then the students write on their hands when they do not know a certain formula, like they do here on Earth. The teacher says: "Let's see what you have on your hand." The moment that what is written on the hand is deleted the knowledge disappears.

So I say, knowledge, which is never deleted from the human mind, is knowledge. Any knowledge, which is deleted from your brain is an illusion of life.

*Book **The First Moment of Love**, lecture "Two Moments"*

When we talk about Love, we understand this: to love constantly. To love is to make a connection with God, Who will teach you the meaning of all things that exist, to understand.

*Book, **The First Moment of Love**, lecture "Two Moments"*

The Lord has created the Earth, but we do not like it. The Lord finds that everything that He has made is very good, but we find that the Earth is not good, therein lies our mistake.

1, p. 234

There is a lack of faith in people, they think about who will take care of them in old age. I ask, Who is taking care of the Earth? Isn't the Sun taking care of it? Man must think for the present day, from morning till sunset; then each day, within itself, will take care of itself.

1, p. 268

Nature is always on the side of the weak. The world is created from small things, countless small particles; these particles define the beginning of the whole Earth.

2, p. 81

Since you are eating, you have to work; since you are breathing, you have to love; since you are thinking, you have to do the Will of God. If you eat, but do not work, you are making a mistake; if you are breathing, but you do not love, you are in error; if you think, but do not do the Will of God, you err.

1, p. 304

So, I will give you one rule from which to benefit from; put yourself to the test! If you have a desire to serve, you have a future, everything is in the serving, in the work which man has the desire to do. If you do not have a desire to study, you do not have a future. If you do not have desire to work, you do not have a future. If you do not have the desire to serve, you do not have a future.

2, p. 210

There are three things on which our future depends. This must be the magic wand. Keep in your mind nice thoughts, it is the magic wand. When you have a nice thought, it is the magic wand. When you have nice feelings, it is the magic wand. When you have done good deeds, it is the magic wand; the wand of the magician.

2, p. 154

The new in the world is for man to enjoy his mind, to enjoy his heart and to enjoy his will. To enjoy those riches, which have been put there from thousands of generations into the body. To enjoy those feelings, which are put in the heart. To enjoy those thoughts, which are put in seed form, to cultivate them. To become an excellent gardener.

2, p. 156

So, I say, the reasonable man in the worst conditions can overcome his hardships. We need to have critical minds.

What does it mean critical mind? He observes the facts, makes a comparison and then draws an inner conclusion. One inner conclusion, which can contribute to our abilities, to understand those laws through which we can work in Nature.

3, p. 137

So, I say, when people begin to believe in one teaching and to think, that it is the only one, they fall into delusion. The doctors help the world. The teachers help the world. The priests help the world. The mothers and fathers help the world. All people in general help, but for us to think that only the fathers and the mothers will save the world is for us to fall into another extreme.

4, p. 151

The beauty of life lies namely in this, that in accordance with our inner development of the spirit, we will be changing constantly, because, as we see, the creation of the Universe is a process of gradual development in which God is constantly manifested. Thus the nice and beautiful in life is manifested, and in that manifestation we live.

4, p. 147

In the future we will have one science which will have at its disposal such sensitive (photosensitive) plates, such that all the hues of a man's thought will be able to be photographed and then you will know the level of human intelligence.

4, p. 206

How should preaching be done? The Truth must be preached with great softness and full consciousness. When I go to somebody to preach to him, first I must love him, to have all the consciousness in myself, that I have to be in his service and to connect him with the living powers of Nature, i.e., to connect him with the Living Nature. Only then, will I be able to help him. It is not necessary to talk a lot to a man, tell him two words only, but say them in such a way, that whatever you tell him later, he believes you.

4, p. 134

Now Christ says: "For where two or three have gathered together in My name, I am there in their midst." *(Matthew 18: 20)* When the Lord comes among us, first we must correct all of our mistakes. A lie smells very bad to the Lord. You shall clean up this lie. A bad look at someone smells, and one's hatred as well smells very bad to the Lord. When the Lord comes, you have to have one musical hearing, to know His steps. He loves music. Do not allow worrying thoughts into your mind; do not worry over trivial things.

Now, if you were in the School, I would have given you something to do. In this School singing is a must. Now you are learning songs. I have listened to church songs. But the contemporary people do not have songs for awakening one's abilities. All singing is suitable for entertainment, it is good for taking a rest. But there are songs, which when you sing them, they awaken your thoughts for thinking. There are songs, which awaken the nice and the beautiful. There are songs, which when you sing them, they awaken in you the feeling of justice.

3, p. 156

So, when some disciple gets tired from the adversities of life, let him take the violin and play on it to himself or let him sing to himself, so he transforms all of his burdensome conditions. In this way the music is an aid to people in their life. When we sing or play on an instrument, we are in connection with more advanced beings than us. If we want to be spiritual, if we want to be religious, we have to sing and play musical instruments.

    I meet many religious people who do not sing and say: "Only the priest or the singers in the church must sing." It is not like that. Each spiritual man must sing. Every spiritual man must understand music and science very well. He must understand well anatomy, physiology, math and geometry. He must have finished at least eight grades. If now it is not like that, then in the future it will be like that. We have to study! And then it is said, we have to know God. I say, God is light, God is knowledge, God is wisdom, God is truth, God is love. When we enter God, we will find ourselves in one great science. Love is a great science. To love, is a whole science.

4, p. 215

Good is the basic tone in the physical world. Justice is the basic tone in the Spiritual world. Reasonableness is the basic tone of the Mental world; it gives birth to everything.

2, p. 313

Life by itself is the best song. When people on Earth suffer, groan and experience the greatest bitternesses, the angels in Heaven rejoice and experience the biggest pleasure. They rejoice, because they understand the deep meaning of the suffering, they know that in it the blisses of humanity are hidden. This combination between sorrow and joy comprises the inner expression of one's musical playing.

3, p. 95

Even in the greatest sufferings, strive to be quiet and calm in your soul. It is not an easy art to suffer inside yourself and to show your calmness. It is an art to suffer and to say to yourself: "It is not only me, millions of people suffer simultaneously with me." When I am suffering, at the same time an ox is being sold to be slaughtered or a lamb is being slaughtered; a man and a woman are in a quarrel; one has a broken his leg; another one cracked his head; the whole world is suffering together with me. My sufferings are nothing before theirs. Afterward come the scarier, the more terrible sufferings, the moral ones.

3, p.18

If we can endure all the contradictions in life, we are in the Divine Love. May the contemporary religious people explain: Why God, Who is perfect, all wise, has allowed these contradictions? In order that He can test our love. The Lord asks: "After all the sufferings, can you love Me? If you love Me, that means your love is real." Hence if you love Me, after I have given you the greatest blessings, this is very natural. If I do you favors every day and you love Me, that is the order of things.

3, p.18

All these sufferings cannot be removed in no any other way than with Love. Love is the only power that can transform sufferings into beautiful forms.
*Book, **The First Moment of Love,** lecture "Two Moments"*

What is a coincidence? If I pass today by some house, and from it falls some clay shingle and hits my shoulder I will say, "This was a coincidence." Okay. Today this thing was a coincidence. Tomorrow, I pass by the same house and some other shingle falls on me and hits me. I will say, "This is another coincidence." On the third day I pass by the same house and in the same way some shingle falls and hits me on the shoulder, will I say again, that this is a coincidence? No, behind the sequence of these facts there is one great reasonable law, which determines things. If in your life comes some misfortune, these are the clay shingles that fall upon you. The reasonable, the invisible world wants to make you think, to see that there is one combination of things. If you are fired as a clerk, is that a punishment for you? No, this is not a punishment. Since you have come to one higher situation, to one higher consciousness, the invisible world says, "For the interest of this man let him be fired from work, to be left without work on Earth. Let others climb in his place." If you realize that the Great has a hand in this thing, that this is its act, you will find one much greater position than the last one.

4, p. 15

Some people say: "We must not be very learned." No, the opposite is true. We have to be very learned and not only that, but we have to be perfect in our studying. We are not to know everything. I do not claim that, but we have to be perfect in our studying, that means, that what we know, we must apply.

4, p. 6

In Love, everything is beautiful. In it there are no contradictions.

1, p. 261

Love is when you help; if you do not help, this is not Love.

1, p. 261

The dark forces are masters of causing sufferings.

1, p. 257

Now people must raise the new flag of Love (God).

1, p. 257

Love has levels. On Earth it is on one level, but up in the Invisible world, it is on another.
Love in the Old Testament differentiates itself from the Love in the New Testament. There are people who still live in the Love of the Old Testament. To fulfill the Will of God is a manifestation of Love. To work for the Kingdom of God and His justice; this, too, is a manifestation of Love. But to work for the glorification of the Name of God; this is the highest manifestation of Love.

1, p. 261

The children inherit only the physical traits of their parents; as a heredity they receive from the parents the physical and etheric body; but the character, the mental and the feeling traits they bear from their previous rebirth. It is very difficult to transfer from one nation to another in rebirth.

1, p. 306

The very first pedagogic rule which you all must have, regardless and without exception is this one: all men, women, children, brothers, sisters, priests and teachers, is to ask our friend to love God first! Your wife is to love God, this God, Who is not only Light outside, but a Light inside as well; the Living light, that is needed everywhere. Him must she love first. If she loves Him first, then she will love you also. If you want to become an object to your wife, know that you have ruined your happiness. In order to be an object to your wife, you must love, you must understand her soul and to be so careful that you never hurt her feelings with anything.

3, p. 16

I consider heroism of the contemporary people this, to endure their own suffering.

3, p. 16

Now in the contemporary life we believe that God is an idea for us. I ask then, "Why did God, Who is so perfect, Who is all wise, let the contemporary religious people answer, why did the Lord allow all these contradictions?" To test our love. The Lord says: "After I give you, the most horrible sufferings, can you love me? If you love me, this is a true love. Because if I give you the greatest blessings and you love me, this is a natural thing. If I do you favors every day and you love me, this is the order of things."

3, p. 16

Every bird has its own nest. It makes it beforehand and lays in it, her eggs. While some people beforehand, lay their eggs, without having a house. If we apply the bird's law in our life, we will say, "Make a house firstly and then get married." Now people get married without having houses. You do not have even a pit house, you will be going from one house to another and you will be expecting to prosper! It is not the issue for people to multiply, the issue is "people" to be born in the world. The issue is not to give birth to sons and daughters, who will come to indulge in the world, but to be born sons and daughters, who will do the will of God, to honor their father and their mother and to work with reason.

4, p. 99

What is marriage?- A limitation.- Why do people get married? To become conductors of the great Divine life. For the development of the mother and the father is judged by their children. If they cannot give birth to good sons and daughters, what kind of mothers and fathers are they? The parents must be good conductors of the Divine and their children must also be such. What kind of preacher is he, who cannot bring Love among people to whom he preaches to?

What kind of preacher is he, who has turned the people to God, but not their purses? ...... By the word "purses" I mean your hearts. So your hearts must be turned over, but not through force, but by the law of Love. Service and serving others is needed by the contemporary people. Service with Love. Whatever you give, give it with the consciousness, that it belongs to God, but not to you. If you have money, it is not yours. The only thing that is yours is the Love which pours out from your heart. Everything else belongs to God. When you invite somebody to eat with you together at your table, enjoy that he is eating with delight. Do not be worried that he will eat a lot. Give everything with Love, so your giving is blessed.

*Book **Divine and Human World**, lecture "Studying and Serving" 08/28/1940*

If the husband does not love his wife, she must pray that he starts to love God. If he loves God, he will love her, too. If the wife does not love her husband, he must pray that she begins to love God. If she comes to love God, she will love him, too. If your daughters, your sons or your friends do not love you, you must pray they start loving God. If they come to love God, and if you come to love Him you will already have friends in the world, with whom you can share everything in your life.

4, p. 331

The Divine life comes when our consciousness is transfused in God and we live in the Whole and for the

Whole; then we know, that there is another way through which life can be manifested.

4, p. 153

It is said in the Scripture, that we can love God. When? When we do His will. But the manifestation of God's Love will be only when you go in agreement with God. Consequently, if we are in agreement with His way, with His life, with His Truth, He is always listening to us.

4, p. 125

One has to live for God – which is then a consecration of the personality, individuality, soul, and Spirit.

1, p. 281

Beware of the great promises. Where there are big promises there lies evil; where there is the smallest promise, there is Good. Good says: "Prefer poverty, death, just to have the benevolence of God;" evil says: "Prefer glory, greatness, everything in the world is for you."

3, p. 200

Abstinence is the reasonableness in man. He who abstains, ponders with reason, he is not in a hurry, but does not slow the things down either, he does these things, the way they are done in Nature. Limiting the evil in you and encouraging the Good in you, this is abstinence. With abstinence, man is passive towards evil and active towards

Good; that man, who is active towards evil, has no abstinence.

1, p. 284

What is evil? Evil gives birth to poverty. What is Good? Good gives birth to abundance. In every relation the Good helps mentally, spiritually and physically. Evil gradually stumbles and the mental, spiritual and the bodily development of man. Evil is that whatever makes a person stumble. Now do not mix anger with evil; anger is not evil, it is one condition of man. Evil is one working principle; evil has completely different considerations.

2, p. 380

So I say now, Love is revealed to the Christian nations. I feel sorry that the contemporary church and especially in Bulgaria, has not yet applied Christ's teachings. The clergy today can apply it! If they do not apply it, we will apply it. The young generation can apply love! The young are full of strength, love, and reasonableness.

4, p. 166

For a man to understand God's thoughts, he must have a mind as vast as the universe and a heart as vast as the Divine world.

4, p. 166

Accept the Divine in you and leave it to develop on its own. Take in the Divine feelings and let them develop on their own. Perceive one Divine action and let it develop on its own. Let some things develop in you on their own. You are causing harm to yourself when you want to develop these things yourself. Sometimes, you wonder how to love; it is not your business how to love. To love a person means to give to the thirsty a cup of water, this is Love; to tell him one good word, this is Love.

2, p. 461

Now, the Divine is working in the world. The world will not collapse. There are good people everywhere. Do not look only at the bad side in the world. All over the world, everywhere there are good people, in whom the consciousness is awakened. On Earth and in the other world the consciousness of the people is awakening. The consciousness of all is awakening, and when you get discouraged, something inside tells you: "Do not worry, there are good people on Earth and there are good people in Heaven."

4, p. 112

Tithe, this is the seed, which you plant. The meaning is: "Give and it will be given to you!" Give one tenth from what you receive. Six days we will work, one day we will give to the Lord. If you work, dedicate one day for God and then the other days will be blessed. If all people were giving a tithe, there would not be even one poor person, not even one unhappy man. Man shall do the tithe with consciousness.

1, p. 293

The good that you do is what is sewn sown in the field. In the Spiritual world you will give half, the remaining half is for you, but in the Divine world you shall give everything. Give and it will be given to you. God wants you to give one tenth of everything. You shall give also one tithe from the ten minutes. For example, you are a clerk and after you work for ten minutes, you shall reason one minute about the Lord, this is a tithe. Out of ten hours, you shall dedicate one to the Lord, for the one hour you will take no money, you are not to be paid monetarily for this one hour.

1, p. 294

The first important question for you is to find the short way to Heaven; the road to Heaven will take you on the right path. Many ask why they have come on Earth. I say, you have already come, do not ask why you have come, but if you must solve a certain issue, that issue is the following, in what way will you spend your life on Earth; in whatever situation you may be, how to will you deal with the Good and evil? Can you spend your life in this way, as God requires? This is the main thought, with which you must deal with and which you must apply this year in your life. If you solve this issue correctly, you will be able to strengthen yourself.

3, p. 97

Do not put man in the delusional position to think that God is outside of him. Do not put God outside of man. You place God on the right side or the left side; when you put Him on the right or left, you already have a false understanding of God. Those who are in hell, don't they have God? They have.

Those who are on the left side have God in the same way as those who are on the right side. When we want to inculcate higher personal qualities in people, when we want to inspire in them that true inculcation of higher personal qualities, that true idea about God, about the religion, we understand that we have to awaken in them that which lives hidden deep in their souls from time immemorial. God has put something nice in each soul; in each soul there are powers which must be developed.

4, p. 125

Now we will not talk about your hardships; these are of one benefit to you, you will bear them, you shall know it. We will not free you from your hardships; to free you from them means to do you the greatest evil. We are giving you knowledge, opportunities for using those hardships for good. In these hardships are hidden all of your wealth. Somebody says: "May the Lord want to take out this hardship;" do not say it like that, but say," Lord, give me the knowledge to overcome all hardships in my life!" You have special hardships in your life, about which you cannot tell anybody.

4, p. 385

Do not ask from the Lord big things! You always want from the Lord big things and that is why you are losing, but instead you have to ask for the little things!

4, p. 385

Now, when applying one method, second, third, finally when you find yourself in a difficulty, you shall say: "Lord, give me a little warmth, give me a little light!" When you feel it, say: "Lord, let it all be for your Glory!" However, when the hardships and the sufferings come, again you shall say: "Lord, let it again be for Your Glory!" For everything that happens in your life you shall say "For the Glory of God!"

4, p. 385

Now we will do one exercise. Separate yourselves from one another by a distance of at least one meter.
Y ou shall turn to the South and pronounce the formula: "May virtue reign, and may all the bad thoughts in the world disperse!"

You shall turn to the East and pronounce the formula: "May God's justice reign in the world and all injustice disappear in our lives!"

You shall turn to the North and pronounce the formula: "May God's truth reign in our lives and all slavery disappear in our soul!"

You shall turn to the West and pronounce the formula: "May God's Wisdom reign in all of the manifestations of our lives and evil disappear from our way!"

You shall turn again to the East and pronounce the formula: "May the Lord reign, and may the Lord be glorified in all of His Love, Wisdom, and Truth!"

"May the Lord reign in His Love, in His Wisdom, and in His Truth. May we do everything for the God's Glory on Earth!"
Amen!

Lecture, *"For the Glory of God"* (4)

Now for a week do an experiment, when you call to mind the name of God, your condition improves right away. If you are not in a good disposition then when you think about the God of Love, Who has created everything, right away your disposition improves. For His sake you are to be ready to make all the sacrifices. To love God in the given case means to make all sacrifices. You get angry, make one sacrifice, not to get angry. When you are mad, say: "This baggage I give it as a gift."

2, p. 331

We must know which thoughts in us are Divine and which are not, we must know their source, whether they come from above or from below. The Divine thoughts bring softness, joy, peace and light. The gladness and the merriment come from the presence of God in man. Now with this, that you have received, you shall help the others by giving it away.

1, p. 256

If you have in you one bad wish, you must not uproot it, but you shall counter it with some good wish. If you have a thought, which is bothering you do not strive to throw it out from you in a mechanical way, because it will create upon you some harm; if it settles down in your mind, you have to find exactly an opposite one to it, to replace it, in this way you will heal yourself.

4, p. 132

The moods in man do not represent something higher. The life of moods deals with disorganized matter, but the feelings represent an organized life. In the senses there are relations between the living cells. At last comes the third phase of life, the spiritual, the reasonable life in which man's consciousness participates. Consequently, you will firstly pass through the moods, they are the weathervane of your life. Then you will pass through the feelings; they show the quantity of humidity, which must be given to life. Finally the light will come which must exert influence upon everything noble and higher in us.

4, p. 349

When you are getting angry, you produce more electricity, more light. To those people who constantly get nervous, their skin begins to get dry, you touch him, his skin is dry. He must change his way, he must not get angry. However, if he sometimes does not get angry at all, it is moisturized. Anger has meaning when there is evaporation of the extra feelings, then the anger is in its place; when there is no excessive humidity in Nature, anger is purposeless. So, let us substantiate ourselves, sometimes you must get angry, so evaporation of the extra feelings can occur.

2, p. 336

In the end, by what will the smart man will be known? The smart man will be known by the difficult tasks which he encountered and solved in his life.

4, p. 142

I say, man can go to the Sun. How is that possible? For the ignorant it is not possible, but for the smart one it is possible. There are adepts in India who are doing it, they go to the Sun. He who goes to it, his heart stops, his pulse stops. You can stop for half an hour the beating of your heart and to tell this heart after half an hour to start again functioning. It beats because of that vital current, which passes through it, but you can move away this current and the heart stops again, but after half an hour to let the current flow and it will begin lightly and gradually to beat. These are issues, which are denied by the contemporary science, but in the future it will acknowledge them.

3, p. 15

Another principle in life is that all things have a rhythm; as a consequence of this, everything comes in its time. You must not rush, there are incoming tides and outgoing tides in the world. Your happiness, your good will come in its time, if you only have the knowledge and the wisdom.

4, p. 356

In meditation, first stop at the top part of the head. Man's moral feelings must be strengthened, which are put under the rays of the Divine Sun and grow. In the one thousand leaves (crown chakra) are located the loftiest senses in man. When you think about God, the one thousand-leaved chakra gets developed, but you have to know, where your thoughts should be concentrated and where to feel it.

1, p. 286

If you concentrate your thought (when) in the room, you can lift yourself up from the ground four fingers (approx. 3 inches). When you free yourself from all Earthly wishes and only one wish is left, the one of Love, you will move away (uplift yourself) four fingers from the ground. This is a great achievement, to be able to uplift yourself four fingers from the ground. Even if you can lift yourself one finger up from the ground, this shows that your mind is very strong.

2, p. 119

Love that does not leave people is a true Love; this Love, that leaves them, is not Love. This that remains with man throughout all conditions and in sufferings, and in joy, and in difficulties that is Love; the only thing, that does not leave man is Love. If you acquire Love, you will have all the power in the world. Love is the magic wand. Some want me to tell them in what lies the magic. Love is the magic wand, with which whatever you say, happens. You must attract it; it is not given, it is not taken, it is attracted, Love can only be attracted. Very little is required for that.

2, p. 196

When we have the principle of Love in us, we will attract all people towards us. This principle is one and the same everywhere and acts equally and in the angels and in man. Do not mix Love with what people call passions.

4, p. 81

Always at the border between two cultures, old and new, crisis appears, great contradictions appear, storms, shocks, catastrophes, because both currents, the old and the new, come into collision, one is getting destroyed, but the other is being built. After these events the bad people will be removed from Earth. She (Earth) is already climbing up and the people with the old understandings will not be able to go up together with her; Earth will shake them down from herself, as the tree shakes itself from the rotten fruits and they will go to another place; they will fall behind in Nature.

1, p. 76

Now comes the nicest world. In the future it won't be allowed for unprepared people to reincarnate, it will be banned to have criminal spirits to come on Earth. They will incarnate in another place, but here, only those who are good and have Love.

1, p. 76

Now the Astral world is being reconstructed. In the past all the evil has been there and it has been the battlefield, but the Earth has been the rear for evil. *(Note, it seems that "rear" has the military meaning here. The army has a rear where all of its supplies and other helpful things are held.)* Now the Astral world is being cleansed, the Earth is becoming the battlefield, but under the surface, Earth is becoming the rear.

1, p. 287

In Christ's coming we understand the manifestation of Love, the Divine principle, which will become a condition for the development of humanity.

4, p. 110

We know that the greatness of any nation, the greatness of any culture can be preserved only when this nation or culture is in compliance with the laws of the Living Nature and when they go in unison with God's commandments and precepts.

4, p. 116

Eliminate all of your negative thoughts and actions towards people, forgive all people, forgive everyone. Each one to forgive his brother and to have full repentance for his ill deeds, God expects this. Then man will be shielded and protected.

1, p. 78

Man has two souls. One is corporeal; it holds everything bad in itself: hatred, malice, selfishness, it is black like coal. The other soul is bright like the Sun. These two souls have a connection between themselves and are always at fight with each other; as they call it, fight between the Spirit and the flesh. The one that prevails, manifests its qualities. When we talk bad (hurtfully), the black soul is manifested; when we talk good, the move to the white soul is given. An inner connection is needed between all souls who are awakened. There must be one inner connection among all awakened souls.

1, p. 309

The words "became flesh," *(John 1: 14)* up to now there is an argument in the Christian world over this verse. It is said in the Scripture: "The flesh and the blood will not inherit the Kingdom of God." *(Corinthians 15: 50)* That means the spirit and the flesh in man are in a fight with each other. The word "flesh" has a few meanings, but because of the lack of other words, this one is used. If the spirit is in a constant fight with the flesh, I ask: why has the reasonable Word become flesh, why choose specifically the form of the flesh? In the word "flesh" we understand living beings, which constantly grow and develop, because there is also flesh which constantly decomposes. Consequently, when it is spoken, the spirit is in a fight with the flesh, it is understood with that flesh which decomposes.

4, p. 291

The Divine man must rule, and the man of the flesh must submit to the Divine man. You will say to yourself: "Listen, you will live and go by the laws of God, thus, as He has ordained! If you listen to Him, you will be able to do anything." With God we can do anything; when I say it like that, I understand that a man who is connected with God, can set his life right. With our present condition there is nothing better than this to set right our lives and to achieve inner peace and knowledge.

4, p. 161

Until God's Love and God's Spirit fill up man, he is a stranger, he is like a foreigner on Earth; he resembles the hungry man who has not eaten and now expects one good lunch.

We will thank God for the nice day, for the sunrise, for the Divine Spirit who comes down and incarnates in people. God has made up His mind to save the whole world, to establish peace and order in mankind, to put light in the minds of people, so the human selfishness is stopped and all people to start living in love, but not as they have lived up to now in war.

Book, **The Two Divine Visits,** Lecture *"The Two Divine Visits"*

When you love, do not be interested in whether they love you. Leave this question unsolved, because to love depends on you, but to be loved, does not depend on you. Sometimes people want to impose on us to love somebody, this, even with an order, cannot happen. You shall love somebody, who needs you. He is hungry, give him a little bread; he is thirsty, give him a little water; he has no clothes, dress him up. You can do him thousands of favors, but you want to tell him: "I love you, love you, love you ... " this is a theater.

1, p. 262

This devil, with whom people are fighting, is not from yesterday. There is one thing with which we can defeat him and that is not to tell a lie, absolutely not to tell any lie. Only he, who does not lie and who has Faith, will be a strong man. However, research the history of the great people, and you will see that they have started with this rule: "Without any lie!" When the lie disappears from us, or we take it out, we will feel an inner freedom, and our mind will begin to work better.

4, p. 165

I say, there are two principles in the world which people must apply in their lives, so they will not be ordinary, but rather a genius. Firstly, they must have unwavering Love towards God, to love Him, without anyone knowing it; and secondly, every lie from their hearts and minds be absolutely excluded. You will say, "Can it be without a lie?" It can be without a lie, a lie must be left outside of life. I am talking about the consciousness of man, in it must not be allowed any lie, neither white, nor black.

4, p. 272

If you want to check out one law, decide in yourself to speak the Truth, not before people, but in your consciousness. Your consciousness must be awakened; never allow yourself to tell a lie. Make an experiment for one month and see what change will happen in your spiritual life. You will see how Heaven will look upon you. Now you are waiting for Christ to come. There, where there is a lie, Christ's foot won't step, this you should know. Why? So, even if freedom comes, it will not benefit you.

4, p. 164

Each one of you who wants to understand the sufferings of Christ, must definitely acquire inner humility. The Scripture says: "God lives in the souls of those who have humility." You must understand humility in depth and its life-giving force. To be humble means to realize, that you can do anything, but at the same time to be so kind that you give way even to an ant.

4, p. 374

In my opinion, the greatest quality that a man can possess is humility. It is not a weakness. The humble man is the most elastic, the most flexible man in the world. Everything that is put on him to bear, endures and poverty may come and diseases may come and death may come (for the humble one there is no death), but I say, that whatever may come on the head of the humble one, he is always quiet and calm, he endures everything. This is the true man. He says, "God, Who lives in me, cannot die; God, Who lives in me cannot become poor; God, Who lives in me, a slave he cannot become; God, Who lives in me, cannot lose strength, cannot get discouraged, nor fall into desperation. Even if they tie me up ten times, even if I am put in jail, when I say: "Lord!", all these ropes will fall down right away."

4, p. 160

Remember that Earth is a place for testing! Here people come to be probed; Earth is a probing place. When they want to test the greatest people in Heaven, they send them here. Your patience will be examined, your mind will be scrutinized, your virtue will be probed, your learning, your knowledge, your art, in music will you be probed, everything must go through these tests in the world and only that which is probed (successfully), remains in the human consciousness. When you go to the other world you can work. That which is not probed is lost. The way they study now in the gymnasiums, how is it? They finish their work in the gymnasium and forget all the formulas, they forget history, they forget many dates. Knowledge that is forgotten, art that is forgotten, music that is forgotten, what kind of knowledge is that?

3, p. 185

Good is the Divine order, evil is the human order. Love is the Divine order, lovelessness is the human order. The lack of faith is the human order, having Faith is the Divine order. Hope is the Divine order, hopelessness is the human order. Now we are misleading ourselves and say, "There is no hope" - this means you have entered the human order. "What must I do?" You will get out of the human order and you will enter into the Divine.

3, p. 247

Be careful that you don't talk too much! There are many sisters and brothers, who talk too much about what they are doing. You are destroying your work, when you talk about what you do. You say, "I did this, I did that." You have done nothing; I consider something done when people begin to benefit from the thing that was done. They begin to benefit from my work, then I gain; until then, until people do not make use of my labor, I do not gain anything. You say: "I pray for the people." Leave that aside. You shall do things for which people will benefit.

3, p. 222

The greatest good which man has from God is life. But the greatest gratitude which man can give for this life is work. It is a great law to respect the work of the others. The more careful a man is to the work of the other, the more careful the Invisible world is to his work. He who works, loves. He who understands, lives. He who understands, works. Christ says: "My Father works and I work, too."*(John 5: 17)*

1, p. 241

Nature loves those who work. As long as you are sluggish, you can never be forgiven; forgiveness shows that you have begun with the application. The stumbling blocks and the hardships are given to cure you from the laziness. To free yourself from the condition of sluggishness, this is the meaning of life.

1, p. 305

A man who seeks the greatest comforts has great comfort, but small achievements. The one, who encounters big hardships progresses more than he who has comforts. Now, many do not want to have hardships. A hardship is a pressure.

What would you have done on Earth, if there was no pressure? What kind of cistern could you have made? No water would have been able to flow if there was no pressure. Many of you now are avoiding the hardships. There are certain hardships which must not be avoided.

2, p. 379

Somebody says: "I have neurasthenia." Eat peas! Another one says, "I suffer from hypochondria. "Eat wheat! They say about someone, "This man is a very quick-tempered man." Give him corn to eat! So and so does not like to hold on to his duties. Give him rye to eat; in the rye there is something ideal, it grows high, and when it enters man, it creates a high ideal. The small plants create people with small ideals, but the large plants create people with high ideals. The villagers from the Sofia area must feed themselves only with rye, so they become bigger idealists.

4, p. 348

There are orthodox people on Earth, but which man can be called "orthodox"?

Orthodox is this one, in whose heart lives God's Love, whose mind is predominated with God's light, without any darkness. Orthodox is this one, in whose soul the Truth reigns and is free everywhere; he is not ruled by laws written by people, but from one great, unchangeable law, written in his soul, such a man glorifies God rightly. If you take this meaning of the word, "orthodox," I understand it, but if somebody thinks that he is orthodox just because he can read the Credo, thus anyone can be orthodox.

4, p. 162

The Bulgarian priests must stop burying the dead. Christ says: "Leave the dead to be buried by their closest ones." *(Matthew 8: 22)* If the task of the priest is to bury the dead, I feel sorry for them. When the truth is told to them, they say that I talk against the Church. Against which Church? You have made one building, and you call it "Church." This is not a Church, the Church is something very beautiful. It represents one of the exalted angels; the Church, this is the human spirit, God lives in it. And then all priests, preachers, bishops from this Church will serve the Great, the Elevated, thus you have to understand these great ideas; if you do not understand them in such a way, you will live only in delusions.

4, p. 358

Someone says, "I have to go to church." There is no better church than the open sky. The best candle in the world is the Sun. Is there anything better than going out in the evening and looking at all of God's candles? You pray and feel the presence of God everywhere. What better priest, from the Spirit of God, who starts to speak to you and awaken in you that Divine, sacred feeling of God? Is there anything better than to see God upon the mountain, as Moses saw him?

4, p. 77

You want an extraordinary love, and you don't want the one you love to be loved by anyone else. It is a law, he who loves only one person, has a very weak love, he who loves all has a strong Love. When you love many souls, you have many inflows; when you love one soul only, you have only one inflow.

1, p. 259

The only thing that can save us and keep us healthy, is the law of Love. We have to think about Love, but this love is only the preface. Sometimes you are not satisfied with Love; this love, which you have tried, will contribute and it is preparing you for the future Love, because without this experience, Love will be inaccessible.

3, p. 221

I will define for you, from the new view point, what thing is Good and what is evil. When man sacrifices the Higher, the Divine, for the human, for the lower, this is evil; but when he sacrifices the lower, the human, for the Divine, for the Higher, this is Good.

4, p. 290

You cannot grow without loving humanity.

4, p. 116

Do not allow the different manifestations of human life to trip you! The outside world may stumble, but you should not stumble. You should know that in whatever direction man manifests himself, it is all for the Glory of God. Your missed opportunities, your mistakes represent opportunities for lifting Beings more advanced than you.

4, p. 378

Now do not say: "If it is so, that everything is for the good, let's make mistakes!" No, it is not like that. When you have unintentionally made a mistake, only when you have unconsciously missed something, then and only then, I will tell you not to regret it. That mistake will be used by another Being for good. Know, that as you are on Earth, you will make mistakes, they are unavoidable, but the mistakes must not be made intentionally. The only danger, from the side of the dark brotherhood, lies in this, that they have the task to plant in man a critical spirit, that he does not live well.

4, p. 378

Every man who says that he cannot perceive the Truth or that he cannot do the Will of God, he himself becomes the reason why a barrier is being put between him and God's Kingdom and then the angels cannot take him into this Kingdom. .... It is said in the Scripture: "The sins that you put as a barrier between you and God are so many, that I cannot do the good that you need." *(Isaiah 59: 2)*

4, p. 326

I would like to ask you how would you be able to convince a man that you love him, without telling him that you love him. I will make it easy for you. You want to convince him that you love him. Bring two apples, one of them smaller, the other one bigger; when you go to him, give him the bigger and leave for you the smaller one and let him see for himself. Bring two objects; with only one it will not happen. You want to give as a gift a hat; bring one crumpled hat, the other one being nice and give him the nicer one, but the crumpled hat leave for yourself.

2, p. 393

In prayer in the Spiritual world we understand the studying of the Divine language; prayer is the first method, through which we begin to study the Divine language. When you begin to pray, you are studying the letters, but afterwards the first syllables of the Divine language. If you do not pray, you will never learn It. Someone says: "Why do you have to pray?"; because only through prayer will you learn the Divine language.

4, p. 79

Christ says: "The Spirit is that, which gives life."*(John 6: 63)* This Spirit, sometimes acts inwardly, through our intuition, but sometimes, externally. He warns us through dreams, but sometimes through our friends. In general, He acts from outside or inside, but when we get elevated and begin to understand Him, then comes the so called first initiation, the Spirit now talks in one clearly understood language, in which the words have only one meaning.

4, p. 261

If they ask in what lies the human culture I will say, the human culture strives to acquire the Reasonable and the Eternal life. When this Life is acquired, evil will disappear. The evil, which now exists in us, exists for completely different reasons. The evil and the Good exist simultaneously in all people; man is polarized simultaneously, if his right side is good, the left is bad.

4, p. 229

We want to construct a world without contradictions. It is impossible to be created on Earth a world without contradictions; plus and minus exist. We want to be happy mentally, spiritually and in a physical way; this is impossible with the current conditions; as a result it is impossible. You have to know that if you have a pleasant feeling for one or two minutes, that after each joy can come a change, a change that can be a big disappointment for you. In Nature we have the same law.

2, p. 83

In the human soul God has put all talents; consequently, the soul must be helped to manifest the Divine. The soul lacks nothing. However, conditions must be created so it gets developed, there lies the salvation, there is the freedom; the soul bears the talents.

1, p. 249

Love is the only way! It takes us out of this labyrinth of the present life. That is why we have to have Love towards God, so we can come out onto the safe shore. Be mobile like the water, patient like the wind, fast like the light and firm like the ground.

3, p. 140

    Firstly, man must have the disposition of a child, to study, to have purity. The reasonable child is an emblem of meekness, humbleness, purity and is ready to study. Man, when he becomes a child, is in the Kingdom of God and when he stops being a child, he is not in the Kingdom of God.

1, p. 298

    On the beaten tracks it is easy to walk, but on the road that is now been paved, walk only the heroes.

3, p. 95

    The scripture says: "Do not cause grief to the Spirit of God, by whom you were sealed!" *(Ephesians 4:30) "And do not grieve the Holy Spirit of God, by whom you were sealed for the day of redemption.")* What should we understand from this verse? When the human enters us we immediately cause grief to the Divine. Is that man smart, who for the human, sacrifices the Divine? He is not smart. The love of God and the human love differentiate in the following, the Divine Love includes in itself everything. In order for your love to be perfect, you must love all simultaneously.

4, p. 81

    You must love not only your neighbors, not only yourself, but all beings in the whole world, about which your consciousness must be awakened at each moment; then only will you feel one inner joy.

4, p. 81

It is bad when people die prematurely, because if he dies prematurely the man must remain here until his years are filled up; for example if he dies 20 years earlier than he should have, he must remain here for the additional 20 years. So, when a man departs on time, he is untied. If he remains here, he will enter into one person or another.

1, p. 235

The world will be set right when God incarnates Himself and begins to live in all people. The way, as it is right now, it cannot be set right, because God is not in all people. He works within the people, but does not live in all of them, because they have not accepted Him from inside. People do not do the Will of God, but instead commit crimes and then ask why the Lord has made it like that. However He reminds them: "Listen to My Will and you will be happy."

1, p. 84

I say, each one must work to re-create himself, this is our task on Earth. If a paint artist comes, he will not be born with his genius, but he is born with all opportunities and gradually, as he works, he becomes a virtuoso in this area, to paint. This is how it happens with the musicians, writers, with the speakers and workers as well. The religious people say: "It will come from the Spirit." It will come from the Spirit, but God wants work.

3, p. 182

Life is defined strictly mathematically. He who is interested in life, must know, that it is a strictly defined mathematical quantity. The true life is that one which emerges from the Spirit.

4, p. 242

Look that you love more and more people, bugs, grasses and flowers, love more and more beings, expand the Love. You will develop one intensive desire to love the whole life. When you have Love towards the whole life, then you will be strong in the Divine Truth. Life, that fills out everything is God's life. You all shall strive to acquire the complete life of immortality. The all-embracing, Love brings the full life.

1, p. 304

Today, people do not understand the sufferings. The sufferings are a forward or one eternal harmonious life. If you understand that in the sufferings is hidden one Divine good and that God's Spirit talks to you through them, a long time will not pass and to you will come such good, which no one will be able to take away from you. In you will be developed one gift, one talent. You could have been the most simple man, some plower or cowman, but if the Divine Spirit pays you a visit, from you will come out something. This we see in the Scripture how David after the visit of the Spirit, from an ordinary cowman became a prophet.

4, p. 85

PaneurHythmy is not an ordinary dance, in its movements are implanted the ideas, which today build and construct the New Culture. In its movements are hidden springs with magical power, through which will be activated the creative powers of the human soul; powers, which are waiting for their development. The Universal Brotherhood brings in the New in the world, not only through thought, feelings and actions, but also through movements.

1, p. 34

If you put in your mind the thought to live for yourself only, you have already set the beginning of your death. If you put in your mind the thought to be glorified, you have set the beginning of your death or the beginning of your misfortune. If you put in your mind the thought to be "strong," you have set the beginning of all disturbances. There is no need for you to strive to be strong; man who lives with God is strong. Man, who lives with God, will be reasonable as well. This now is a logical understanding.

4, p. 157

Somebody says, "Why did I come into the world?" You are one element in the world, and you must live for the glory of God. Did you finish your job as such an element? In the morning, when you get up, how many good thoughts pass through your mind? Did you fulfill at least one of these thoughts? Throughout the day you were presented with thousands of opportunities to do a good deed, did you do at least one? Just talking about doing something good is not enough, but rather doing good is what matters. *(Acts 10: 38)*

4, p. 139

We now want to be strong, learned and rich, but we want these to be for our personal benefit; there lies the whole mistake. You want to be spiritual for yourself, but you must be spiritual for others. The mistake of the whole world lies in this, that God's invested capital is scattered, it is not processed.

1, p. 235

Evil lies in this, when man lives exclusively for himself only and forgets to live for others. However, with Good, man lives for others.

1, p. 237

Let's discuss the basic things. You shall have an idea what is able to change your conditions; in this meaning you must first understand the idea of Love.

When it is about Love, be ready to make all sacrifices. Here is what I understand, in the given situation, when Love comes, be ready to become Its servant, whatever It wants from you, you must do it, never refuse what It wants from you. You will now think, that It will ask from you your house. Your house It will not ask for, It will ask for such a small thing, that you will see it as funny, that It deals with such childish things.

2, p. 331

Now the Lord says: "I will show him how much he must suffer for My name." To suffer for God's name, this is the ideological idea inside a man's life. A man who cannot suffer for his ideas, does not understand the meaning of life.

3, p. 13

Our consciousness must be awakened. You say, that you love somebody. I ask you, "Do you love God?" You say: " We love Him, we strive to love Him." No, when I talk about God, I must be ready to sacrifice everything, to be free from everything in the world. If I love God, I will love all people and I will be able to cope with all people. If I do not love God I cannot love my fellow man as well, I won't be able to even cope with myself. A man, who does not love God, is the biggest egoist, and he cannot live with anybody.

4, p. 331

The scripture says: "No one lives for himself." The biggest mishap is when we think, that we live for ourselves. Everyone who has tried to live for himself has ended up catastrophically: the part outside of the Whole has no meaning. We, as a part of the Whole, are rays, that have emerged from the Great.

4, p. 211

Life is one, physical, spiritual and Divine. When man does not understand life, for him it is only physical; when he half understands it, for him it is spiritual; but when he understands it completely, it is Divine.

1, p. 246

I say, some of you now are sitting at a crossroads and are thinking over which teaching in the world is the right one. The teaching which gives an expansion to your soul, an expansion to your mind and an expansion to your heart, that teaching is a Divine one. The teaching which brings, every day, this Divine nectar of life, the teaching that brings into you the impulse to overcome all hardships and to grow, that teaching is a Divine teaching. The teaching with which you do not grow old, do not lose the meaning of life, but every day you are rejuvenating, enriching yourself and growing, this is the Divine teaching.

4, p. 113

The advanced Beings work upon our culture and upon our souls. They will produce in us the new man, they will prepare us for the new life, of which we have no idea. The exalted conviction, which man has, is given from the Divine world to man as a gift, in whom God trusts; one conviction is given to him, which cannot be vanquished.

1, p. 290

True happiness is in God. If you return back to your Home, with your consciousness you will feel the oneness or you will experience nirvana. Nirvana is the place, where the oneness of things can be felt. If you go into nirvana, you will understand that certain causes give certain consequences; then you realize that this road which you have passed, is the best. Now no one can convince you in this, only in nirvana you will be convinced, that this road that you have passed is the nicest.

1, p. 267

We have to acquire one quality of light, selflessness and one quality of the water, softness. I call the generous man, water; but the man who gives knowledge to people, light. I wish that you be generous and to give knowledge to people and in this way to form those wonderful and good connections, which will make you, in the future, brothers on Earth and brothers in Heaven.

4, p. 25

Humility is a movement towards God; pride is a movement towards matter. In pride, man has formed his body; in humility, he has formed the love towards his neighbors. The good and the humility together form the movement towards God. A man, who is not good and humble, simultaneously, cannot move towards God.

2, p. 257

Till now you have thought that humility is climbing down. With humility, you are not climbing down, instead you are climbing up. With humility the only situation is to climb up. In climbing up, man has acquisitions. No one, so far, has clarified humility in this way. You, up to now, have not understood humility, as climbing up. The humble one thinks about God; he is climbing up. The proud one does not climb up, he thinks about other things. The mind and the heart are climbing up with humility.

2, p. 248

When you are discontented with life, this condition is pride; when you are contented with life, this is humility. Have this understanding, humility is a movement upward, pride is a movement downwards. Good is the situation which crosses both movements. There, where the humility begins and there where pride stops, are the two end points of the Good, thus we have one triangle. Humility ends where pride begins.

2, p. 249

Let's assume that you have a quadrangle. In a quadrangle are the worst conditions. In order to get out of them, you must draw two diagonals, to find the center of this quadrangle. Only by inner roads can you overcome the outer hardships. This square you must rotate around its axis, so as to form a circle. The circle is a condition so as to change the outer conditions which are tightening around you. You ask, "How will I make the circle?" You will form it around yourself. We say "society." Man must create a good environment around himself, with good people, who will help you in your work.

2, p. 375

If you say that you can do anything, without having God in mind or His Spirit, you have taken the wrong path. Moses, one time only, allowed himself to say: "Can I not draw water from this rock?" and could not enter the Canaan land. Moses was a great prophet, but only because of these words, which he directed towards the Jews and did not glorify God, he separated from the Whole and could not enter the Canaan land. I say, if Moses slipped and could not enter the Canaan land, how much more can one ordinary man slip! **Therefore, in whatever situation you are in, you shall say, "Lord, you can do anything! And Your Spirit, Who comes out from You, can do anything. And I, through the Spirit, Who leads and directs me, can do anything!"**

You ask me: "When shall we pronounce this formula?" When you find yourself in the most difficult situation. Pronounce this formula, once, twice, three times until you win.

3, p. 106

With running away, the issues are not solved. Where are you going to run to? To go to God, I understand that. Abandon the running away, but say to yourself, **"No matter how difficult this work is, I will do it with God and with the Spirit, who leads me."** Therefore, with all the difficulty conditions in your life, use this formula.

3, p. 106

The story about the prophet, Daniel, in the pit with lions is one of the most famous subjects and if we stop at its inner interpretation, we will understand, that the prophet Daniel or the righteous people, will be put among the manifestations of the animal beginning or the bad conditions, but they will be saved. *(Book of Daniel, Chapter 6)* The animal, the rude and lower beginning in man is tame only when from inside is manifested the Divine beginning.

Each mystical verse in the Bible has seven interpretations, and all of them are true. Always seek at least the three important interpretations, which are for the physical, for the Spiritual and for the Divine world; each one of them is true, but one from another is deeper. Whatever is outside is inside as well; whatever is inside is outside as well.

1, p. 312

The spiritual man first spiritually cleanses himself from the inside and then cleanses the outside, but the secular man first cleanses himself from the outside and leaves for later to cleanse himself on the inside. *(Luke 11: 39)*

1, p. 308

The true understanding of life lies in the Love of God. The Love of God is the beginning of things. The love towards a neighbor, this is the solution of things. In this solution, Love is the cause. The love for yourself is the last thing to consider. If the lives of the contemporary people do not go as they should, it is because they have turned this law into the reverse. The love for yourself is a consequence of the other two types of love. Love towards a neighbor is the cause, but the Love towards yourself is the consequence of this, but the Love of God is the beginning, from which all other things emerge. So, the Love, the love for yourself is the result, the consequence, the last thing. People have reversed this law, they have abandoned and put in the background the Love of God and their neighbor, but the Love for themselves they have put in the first place, as a result of which there is a division among people. People cannot agree with each other, because everyone pulls his purse, his towel or his bag always towards himself.

5, p. 11

This teaching has an application in the contemporary life of people. In order for man to be healthy on Earth, to be strong and to do his work as needed, Love definitely must reign in his soul. In order to foresee things about to happen, to know what will happen in the future, Wisdom definitely must reign in his mind; but to be strong and to be free, the Truth definitely must reign in his spirit. This is the way. If, in the man's spirit reigns Truth, if in the man's mind reigns Wisdom and if in the man's heart reigns Love, the man's life is definitely set right. Then people's life will not be like the present day's life. And then man not only will be healthy, but will be beautiful, will be blessed and happy in himself.

5, p. 12

Many of the contemporary secular people sit and seek the Lord, asking themselves where is He, on heaven or on Earth? They read some books, what some authors wrote about Love, they seek It in books. The Lord is not some outer object to have the need of proof. He is not in time and space, He is outside of time and space. He is not something physical. When you love somebody, can you tell the people where your Love is? Can you show It to them? Love is not something external to be seen or be touched. You, have you seen the Love? Somebody can give you a hug, but hugging is not Love. Love is not something visible. Even when they say for a man, that he thinks and the thought is something invisible. Love is invisible, but is real; thought in the same way is invisible, but is real. When Love enters some man, who has been rude, cruel, or ferocious, he right a way becomes soft, ready to do any favor and make any sacrifice. But when Wisdom enters a man, who has been ignorant, who did not know how to act, it makes him right a way reasonable man, he knows already how to act, he is ready to do anything. Such a man becomes learned. This man already can become a musician, painter, sculptor, he can become whatever he wishes. Now I recommend you to turn your attention to this, which God has put in you and to work upon it.

5, p. 13

So, when people ask how can their lives be set right or improved, I say, people's lives can be improved, when Love comes to reign in their hearts, when Wisdom reigns in their mind and when the Truth reigns in their spirit.

5, p. 14

When man makes the decision to do the Will of God, then the new life will come in him. Then all hardships, sufferings, contradictions, misunderstandings, misfortunes in life will disappear. Man will be freed from slavery and will enter into freedom. This is what Christianity states in the new meaning. That is why people must free themselves from the old life and to enter the new one.
"Everything in life is achievable."

5, p. 14

Having power is dangerous when you do not have Love in you; strength is dangerous, when you do not have knowledge, strength is dangerous, when you do not have the

Truth in you. Wealth is dangerous, when you do not have Love, when you do not have knowledge, when you do not have the Truth in you. Everything in the world is dangerous without God's Love, Wisdom, Truth and knowledge.

5, p. 30

We want the Will of God be done, but we are waiting for others to do it. Each one of us must be a conductor of God's Will. However, can I set the world right? There is no need for you to set the world right, you have to only become a conductor of God's Will. If you become a conductor, you will uplift yourself. This must become a condition for your soul to be uplifted. Your soul must be uplifted to a higher level and to be enriched in knowledge, in strength and in virtues. The sufferings and the tests that you are going through, they are temporary.

5, p. 33

While you are on Earth, you must roll up your sleeves to work, you must become servants and when you get there, for where you are preparing yourself to go to, you will be met like princely sons. On Earth you cannot bear kingly titles and crowns. Here you will wear a little bit of torn clothes, with patched footwear and clothes. You say: My shoes are broken. I prefer to wear broken shoes, but moreso my heart to be pure, than to be with patent leather shoes, but my heart be impure. I prefer to have a bright and enlightened mind, than to wear a leather coat with a sable collar and cylinder hat on my head.

5, p. 34

Always keep your brain in order. Keep in order your sympathetic nervous system, which is connected with your feelings and with your heart. The brain system is connected with your thoughts. Consequently, whatever negative thoughts come to you, that this or that happened, say to yourself: "Everything is for the good." When something happens with your feelings, say, this is for the good. Somebody died, it is for the good. Somebody has been suffering, it is for the good. Whatever may happen to you, know that it is for the good. If you become poor, you have freed yourself from one headache. Somebody has become rich, may the Lord help him to carry his burden.

5, p. 35

Adam and Eve lived in Paradise with all the good conditions at their disposal, and had access to all the good things of Paradise; they lived like princes, so why did they sin and why did they die? I ask, what is the reason, that they lost paradise? You will say that they sinned. The sin is one of the reasons, but why did they sin? Sin is due to what? The sin entered from the weak spot, it started from the heart, and then came to the mind. Whereas neither the heart can withstand the pressure of the sin, nor the mind can withstand the pressure of the crime. Consequently, the first humans were banished from Paradise because sin entered there. So, because of these two specific reasons, man was kicked out banished from Paradise, for the sin of the woman and for the crime of the man. The sin came through the heart, through the woman, but the crime, through the man, through the mind. Now the whole human race is being inculcated with higher personal qualities with the goal of setting right its heart from the sin and its mind from the crime.

5, p. 47

I ask, to what are due the sufferings? Through the sufferings, the human heart is straightened out. This is from a pure pedagogical point of view and from nature's point of view. The human heart cannot be straightened out in no any other way except through sufferings. In order for the human heart to be straightened out, to come to its normal condition, it must go through the sufferings. Why is man being punished? So that his mind is straightened out. Consequently, the heart cannot be straightened out without sufferings, and the mind cannot be rectified without punishments. That's why it is said, for whom the Lord loves, He punishes. The man is punished, but the woman suffers, she is put to sufferings.
(Note: Oftentimes the Master used symbols and symbolic language in his lectures, I think the Master spoke with symbols in the last sentence as well.)

5, p. 47

So, what is wealth? Wealth is a conductor in the world. You must not use your brain for the gaining of wealth. You must use your mind for doing favors to people. Wealth is given to man to do favors with it to others as well, it is not given just to him and his children. To think like that is a wrongful understanding of the law. The rich are a cashier of God, Who will call him tomorrow to give an account. You ask, how is that? We inculcate higher personal qualities in our children, we give them education, they finish universities. In my opinion, only he who has learned the way of good, the way of knowledge, the way of truth and freedom, only he has finished the university.

5, p. 48

Nobody has the right to complain, that he does not have a good wife. When God led Adam into Paradise, He did not tell him, "Here is the woman." Whereas He told him, "I will make you the woman a helper in your life." The woman is the helper of man. She is the heart that beats. The man must protect this heart. He must find one heart and to measure it, to see whether it is for him. People are amazing when they want to marry. If somebody wants to get married and comes to me, I will tell him, the woman is one heart which must correspond exactly to yours, it must conform to your rib, which God has taken in the past. You must find this heart, which fully pulses with your mind. If the heart of a woman does not pulse equally with the mind of her husband, this woman is not for that man. If the mind of a man does not give an impulse to the woman, this man is not for that heart. This must be known by all, so as not to mislead themselves.

5, p. 51

Inasmuch as Christ's teaching is applied and tested by the people, it does have meaning. You say, Christianity. In what lies Christianity? Christianity lies in the fraternization of people. First, all people must fraternize.

5, p. 69

If you do not love the man, who you see, how are going to love God, Whom you do not see? You ask, in which direction is God? Everywhere, where people are reasonable. There, where people are foolish, God is not there. God is in the pure life. His, thought, His power, His presence is there, where the people are reasonable and live a pure life. If you are understanding it like that, He is everywhere. He is nearby and far away.

5, p. 69

Create for yourself one faith, that cannot be changed by anything, that nothing can limit it. You must develop such a faith in yourself, which in all cases remains faithful and not to change. Faith must be put to the test. Somebody says that he was told one bitter truth. The Truth is never bitter. There is nothing sweeter than the Truth. The Truth is the ultimate limit, the ultimate goal. Behind the Truth you cannot go. Behind the Truth is the death, behind the Truth is the suffering. Now you are behind the Truth. You ask, what thing is the Truth? This, that brings knowledge, happiness, strength, life, wealth, this which brings everything in the world, that thing is the Truth. But what is there behind the Truth? There is nothing behind the Truth. Consequently, I consider, that Love is the beginning of life, but the Truth is the end of life. These are the two limits of the Great in the world. This, that moves in the middle and forms the things, that is knowledge, that is the Divine Wisdom. You cannot have Wisdom in the world, if you do not have a beginning and an end. Between these two points must be filled the innerspace of eternity. So, Wisdom fills the life. The Wisdom clarifies what thing is

Love and what is Truth. You say, lets love each other. This is the beginning of life. To speak the Truth, this is the end of life. If you do not have knowledge, if you do not have Wisdom in life, all other things will remain meaningless. Consequently, if you, with your Love, cannot pass from one end of life and enter into the Truth, and if you, with your Truth, cannot enter from the end into the beginning of life, you do not understand what thing is life.

5, p. 80

So, I say, till you, in your misfortunes do not strive to help other people in their misfortunes, you will not be able to escape the poor situation you are in. This law is true and for the families and for the societies and for the nations, it is present almost everywhere. They call this an altruistic feeling. Somebody asks, why should I help others? If you help others, you will help yourself.

5, p. 91

"Everything is possible." When? When you act in accordance with the Divine. How can one figure out which act is Divine? When a man does not think for himself, but thinks for others, this act is Divine. This man always acts Divinely. Whereas when a man thinks for himself, he always commits a crime. Why does the wolf commit crimes? Since he thinks for himself. Why does the eagle commit crimes? Since he thinks for himself. We will see, that all crimes in the world are due to those conditions, in which man thinks only for himself. Man thinks that after his life is arranged well, everything else will be arranged as it should. Yes, but tomorrow somebody comes along stronger than him and sacrifices him. That is how you act, too. You enter the chicken coop, you catch one hen, but she starts screaming. You cut of her head and thinking nothing of it. If you think in accordance with God, you will say, let this hen live. How should you act? You catch the hen, cut off her head and tell yourself, she is a hen, she must die so that I can live. I can give you many of examples about the bad consequences which man bears for his unjust actions. I was told a story which happened in Sofia. A butcher wanted to cut the throat of a bull to kill it; for a whole hour he was cutting its throat, but could not kill it. Finally, out of anger, he put him on the ground, plucked out one of its eyes and thus he managed to skin its skin. Within a week, another bull kicked him in the same eye. Thus the butcher lost one eye.

5, p. 91

In what lie the principles of freedom? If I act unfairly towards people, I am not a free man. If my thought produces anxiety, I am not a free man. If my disease is paralyzing me, I am not a free man. But man must be free. Yes, man must be free in mind, heart, will and by health.

5, p. 91

"Everything in God is possible." Everything is possible for he who believes in God. Everything is possible for him who loves God. Everything is possible for he who studies the laws which God has set in the world. Everything is possible for he who loves the Truth.

5, p. 102

Who is a righteous man? A righteous man is he, who is connected with Love, with the eternal beginning. A righteous man is he, who is guided by the law of Love. When man has the Love in himself, he is so rich, that he does not need to take anything from anybody. Consequently, the righteous man can never commit a crime, because he himself has everything and gives from himself. The crime comes only from the lack of things. He who wants only to take, he commits crimes. This fact has already been checked out. Eve sinned because she wanted to take one fruit from the forbidden tree. Adam and Eve had everything at their disposal, but wanted to become richer than what God made them and because of that they sinned. This is an interpretation, but whether it is the cause or not is another issue. The fact is, we are out of Paradise.

5, p. 110

Everyone in whatever nation he lives, must be the bearer of the new views of Love. Love is the carrier of the true freedom. With Love there is a choice, but in the old philosophy, there are no choices. You say, this is my debt. If it is your debt, you cannot be free, you must pay it. Freedom in the world can only come with Love.

5, p. 134

Now if we want to be favorable to God, if we want to have a positive credo, we all must serve to that positive Divine Love. To that Love, which will bring peace in your souls, which will bring light in your hearts, which will bring health, it will improve the situation in families, it will arrange our lives everywhere. Your life cannot be arranged in no any other way, but only through Love. So far in my scientific research I have not been able to find other methods through which man can be inculcated with higher personal principles. No matter how much you inculcate man with higher personal principles, he will still remain un-inculcated with higher personal principles. The only method in the world, which can improve man, which can inculcate him with higher principles, is with unobstructed Love. To let man be absolutely free. Do not hold him accountable, leave it to others to hold him accountable. This man does as much as he can bear. If you have a horse, do not load him with more than he can carry, do not load your mind with unnecessary things, because we should not want to solve issues which are unneeded. Now our mind is not in the condition to solve these issues. If you want to solve this issue, you can solve it easily. Put yourself in a calm condition, and you will transfer yourself in a dream, where you will see how the issue is resolved. These issues have been solved long ago. When Moses wanted to build a tabernacle to Jehovah in the desert, God took him to the other world and told him to make the tabernacle exactly as he saw it. There, in the other world, he saw the built tabernacle with all the exact dimensions, so the architects were able to make it accordingly.

5, p. 135

"Life is more precious." When? When Love acts in it. When Love does not act, there is no greater burden in life for a man. That is why the Indians, who have studied life without

Love, as well as Buddha, have said, that man must free himself from life. Buddha is right, man must free his present abnormal life, but to receive, as Christ has said, the eternal life. Or, this is eternal life, truly to know God. God, Who lives in us, and we must be one with Him.

5, p. 137

I say, the kernel of my teaching (in other places, the Master said that it was not his teaching, it is God's teaching, since there is only one Master-God) are Love, Wisdom and Truth. Then they ask me, tell us what is this thing Love, what thing is Wisdom and what thing is the Truth? I say, Love is this without which cannot exist any life. Wisdom is this without which no movement exists. Truth is this without which no border exists. The Truth is the last borderline of Genesis. Everything that is created, as it walks and walks, at the end it will stop at the Truth. You can walk for thousands of years, but when you come to the Truth, there you will stop. The Truth is the last boundary of each direction. When you come there, one of two things will happen: you will either take into consideration the laws of the Truth and live according to them; or you will turn into dust and ashes. Somebody says, tell me the Truth. The Truth cannot be said, it is lived.

5, p. 139

The Truth represents entire life. It includes this, in which God is manifested. It includes this, in which all perfect beings are manifested. Truth is the nicest, the most beautiful thing in the world, which has not yet come into the mind of man. It cannot be expressed. It includes all of eternity, which is comprised of thousands and millions of eternities. So, there are eternities that are limited, but there are also eternities which are limitless.

5, p. 139

Everything in the world is subject to evolution. There is nothing in the world which is not evolving. Human thoughts, feelings and actions are subject to a certain evolution. All beliefs, all religions are subject to evolution. The only thing in the world that does not evolve and remains unchanged and is absolute, is God. If somebody says, that religion evolves, you will say that this is a delusion. In my view, if religion does not evolve, that is a delusion. In what do people believe today? The thoughts of people have changed and continue to change. As children, they believed that their dolls were alive; as adults they believe that the dolls are made of wood, human products. The dolls are automatic devices. There are many people who are such automatic devices, which I call people-automatic devices. When I talk about man, I understand this being, which has a spirit, it has a soul, it has a mind, it has a heart, and lastly, it has a will. This is man. That being in which these things are not manifested simultaneously, is some human being, but it is seemingly a man, he is a man-automatic machine. They are of service to humanity, but from a different order of magnitude.

5, p. 142

Every day you should have at least one little change in yourself. Every day you must take in one new idea in your mind.

5, p. 143

People want to be convinced of the existence of God. God is not something that can be proven externally. First of all, God's existence cannot be proven. To prove what God has created I understand; but God Himself cannot be proven. The scientists want to prove the existence of God, but by the way they want to go about it, it is impossible to prove the existence of God. You can prove anything that way, but never the existence of God. Inasmuch as people cannot prove the existence of God in this way, they see that this way is false and they finally say that God does not exist. They are right in one regard, namely that such a God, whatever God they preach about from the outside, does not exist.

5, p. 144

All of you must purify your views in view of your future life. If you do not purify your views, you will not free yourself from your sufferings. This is necessary, because whatever your views and concepts for man are, you will be the first one to benefit from these views of yours. For example, you have one man, one friend of yours, whom you love. The higher your views of your friend are, the better for you as well, because he will be more ready to do you a favor.

The lower your views of him are, the lower will be his ability to sacrifice himself for you. There are people in the world who are ready to sacrifice themselves for their friends.

The same thing can be said for your relationship with God as well.

5, p. 145

You ask, why do we have to love? You have to love, because through Love you are modeling yourself. If you do not love, you will remain a mediocre man, and you will not progress. Progress is only possible with Love. When Love, the fire of the organic development, performs, after, it will perform the Wisdom, and the Knowledge. After the Wisdom will come the Truth and the Freedom. All these things come consecutively, but without the inner Love no change can be made. Many changes can happen in the world, but this, what we want, cannot happen without Love. Everyone who has lived without Love, in the end has gone through disappointments.

5, p. 151

All of a man's misfortunes come through accepting the evil within himself. When he accepts evil in his organism, one compound is formed. Imagine that in a man comes a desire to steal something. It is not bad, that a man wanted to steal 10-15 thousand leva (The plural form of the Bulgarian currency "lev" is "leva.") but this act will leave bad consequences for four generations. After this theft, man must go through four generations, so this impurity can be cleansed from him. Statistics have shown, that one evil is liquidated in four generations, but one good deed done, shows its consequences for thousands of years. In this case it is better for a man to do one good deed. If a man would have done one microscopic good deed every day, he would have great results. If, everyday, the mother, the father, the daughters and the sons would have done one small and good deed, they would have acquired a lot; no other inculcation of higher personal qualities, would be needed. If, every day, the mother, the father and the children would have done one small good deed and in the evening, when they come back home and each one tells to the others what good he has done, to share his experience, there is nothing greater than that.

5, p. 174

I ask, if you dissolve ten cubes of sugar in a kilo of water, what evil have you done? When you evaporate the water, the sugar will separate; it did not get lost. The loss is only in our mind. When we think that there are losses, we live in the human world. The losses remain only in the human world, but not in the Divine. Misfortunes exist only in the human world, but not in the Divine. In the Divine world there are neither losses, nor misfortunes. In the Divine world there are only gains. These two worlds, the human and the Divine, are in contact with each other, but differ from one another completely. It is said in the Scripture Book, that we live and move only in God. Here, every moment, every second, we take from the air, we inhale air, but who from us has been able to hold this air for himself? Who from us was able so far to swallow the air? Whatever quantity of air one inhales, he gives it back.

5, p. 182

Who can be unjustly treated? The weak. The strong can never be unjustly treated. Consequently, when you suffer, you are weak; when they unjustly treat you, you are weak; when you are sick, you are weak; when you make mistakes, you again are weak. When you do not love, when you envy, again you are weak, and you belong to one world, from which you will never free yourself. And that is why I say, until you live in this world, you, as you were born and thus you will die. Anyone, who tells you, that with this understanding of life, you can free yourself, he is not telling the truth.

"The good news!" Where does the good news come from? The good news comes from the Divine world. Then will you be strong, but the strong man has four qualities: he is the man of over-abundant Love; he is the man of over-abundant life; he is the man of over-abundant knowledge and wisdom; he is the man of overabundant truth and freedom. Consequently, man's strength is the result of this, what he has in himself. You say, that it, the strength, can be acquired. If you can acquire it, you will be free; if you cannot acquire it, you will bear your burden and no one will be able to help you. But somebody may pity you. These pities are useless. The good news must show us an exit way.

5, p. 183

It is said in the Scripture: "Soft response." This is that response, which can transform your thoughts and feelings. For example, how can a man free himself from the hatred and to transform it? He will transform it into Love. How will he free himself from the fear? When you transform it into faith. How will you transform that power of destruction? When you

transform it into compassion. This shows that in man there are corresponding places, centers, whose energies can be transformed from one kind to another. When man knows how to transform one energy into another, he will know how to free himself from one misfortune. When it is said, that one man can turn another one to God, this means, that he can transform in that one, certain kind of energies which are for crimes, into higher energies. Truly, in man, there are deposited energies for committing crimes, but with work upon himself he can transform them into a higher condition.
5, p. 185

Until all people desire many things, the world will not be set right. At the moment they stop desiring, the world will be set right. Whatever they have wished is enough. To constantly wish is criminal. Somebody wants to become rich. He gets up in the morning prays to God to give him 500 thousand leva. He sends his application, but the next year he again asks for 500 thousand leva. Thus he continues year after year to ask wealth from God, but God does not answer to not even one of his applications. Why? Once he gives his application, he must leave it and not to mention anything about it anymore. There is no sequence in your actions. You are in consideration that you are in one world, where you have to be constantly asking.
5, p. 188

The difficulty in your life lies not in that you have not asked for as much as you should have, but that you do not know how to ask. If I had come into this world with the knowledge, that I have today, I wouldn't be giving the Lord an application to give me 500 thousand leva, but I would have asked Him to acquaint me with a few good people and they in turn with their friends. If I had come to Earth, I would have asked from God one art: either to carry my violin on my back and be a musician; or to carry my paint brushes for painting pictures in my bag; or to carry in one small bag one small first aid kit with my medications. That is how I would have chosen one of those three professions, but the others I would have put aside, because they are tied with many expenses. If I would have chosen to be a merchant, I would have been carrying whole ledgers, whole books, but that would have cost me a lot.

5, p. 188

In order to love man, he must definitely contain something of value in himself, otherwise you will waste your time in vain. You ask, then how should that religious claim be understood, that we must love all people? I ask, what do you understand in the word, that all people must be loved? Truly, the basic rule is that you must love all people like yourself. Yes, but there is still one difference. Man must make for himself a line of many bendings in order to love all people equally. This is not an easy job. You must be a perspicacious man, in order to find in man that nice thing, for which to love him. In order to love somebody, your Love must be based on something. We say that all people are made by God, but until you get convinced in that thing, a great deal of philosophy is required. Among the people are noticed a line of differences which exists within them. In order to say that all people are made by God, you must live in the Divine world. When you come to Love, the issue is already solved. With Love, we come to the finished results. You cannot not love that apple tree, which has born a lot of fruit, they are ripened and hanging from it. That apple tree, which has not born anything yet, you do not love. Your love for it will be in projection.

5, p. 189

There are people, who are objective, in them their intuition is poorly developed. There are men, who are objective, but often men are subjective. There are men who do not believe their wives, however, when the intuition in the woman is well developed, these men must pay attention to her intuition and listen to her. When she gives her opinion, her opinion is valid. When the issue is about the objective, about the material, there man is strong, and therefore, whatever he says, the woman must listen to his words. The intuition relates to far away future things, which are to happen to man, but the objective mind relates to the close, the material things, which occur in man's life. We must know what is in store for us.

5, p. 189

So I say, people's happiness in this world, depends not as much on themselves, but on the people who love them. You may not agree with this, but I reason a little bit differently. The strength of one knife depends on the blacksmith who made it. The blacksmith has put in the knife certain qualities which determine its strength. The strength of a plough depends again on the blacksmith who made it. Whatever quality the blacksmith has put in the knife, such quality will show. If he who works with the plough, puts it in a hard and a dry ground that it cannot withstand and breaks down, who is the cause of that? The cause is in he, who manages the plough. Then, on the same basis, God, Who has made our world, our body and has put in us many good qualities, is He guilty for the misfortunes that come upon us? The cause for the misfortunes lies in us alone, who are making experiments. I put the plough in a hard ground and it breaks down. We ourselves are at fault, that we do not plough a soft dirt, but instead a hard one.

5, p. 191

Now they say that the poor can easier enter into heaven. We see that and the poor do not go to heaven. In heaven, in that well organized world, in the world of Love go only those people, who fulfill the will of God. The rich who do the will of God go to heaven. The poor who do the will of God go to heaven, too. The poor and the rich people who do not do the will of God, do not go to heaven. It is said that poor Lazarus went to heaven. Lazarus was a humble man, but at sometime in the past he had eaten and had drunk like the rich. That is why when he was sitting at the door of the rich and looking how they were living, he was telling himself, I, too, once upon a time, lived like you, I ate and drank, but now I understand what the meaning of life is. I am content with everything that God gave me. To the dogs, who were licking his wounds, he was telling, "Now you can lick, whatever I have, one day I will leave to you." What happens next? Lazarus dies and goes to heaven. The rich died also and went to a resort, in warm places, there to heal himself. But when he got very hot there, his lips dried up, and he called upon Abraham to send him Lazarus to moisten a little bit of his throat. The issue is not about the outer riches only. We all must be rich, like God is rich. We all must in our actions, be like God. This is the philosophy of life. In God there is one quality, that when He passes by the smallest beings, He stops and renders them a favor. However small they may be, even though they do not know Him, He is always ready to render them a favor.

5, p. 192

Christ says: "If you love me, you will keep my commandments, my law." *(John 14: 15)* What is this law? The Happiness. Man's happiness lies in one thing: to love. When he loves all, this means, that he is happy. To love only in a human way, this means to be unhappy. When we say that we love God, this means, that we love in our souls all beings. This means to love all beings, but not outside of you, but to keep them in your mind and in your soul. You cannot love one being from the outside, which occupies a part, some spot from space. This little being in you, that you love, does not occupy any spot in space. All beings that you love and which exist in God, can be gathered in your brain, in this small country.

5, p. 197

The good news. The Scripture says: "Reconcile!" With who? With the one who loves you. Now it remains for people to study how to reconcile. Reconciliation in the world cannot happen without Love. Man must have knowledge, to understand, whether it is time to reconcile or not. Man must know whether it is time to love others or not. Since Love, too, must come on time and to correspond to the level of the development of each soul. Required are very smart people, who are to love. Since, with his love, man can do the greatest good and the greatest evil. With knowledge it is the same too, man can do the greatest good and the greatest evil. For example, if the knowledge is revealed to him prematurely. Also, in the freedom man can do a great good, but also a very big evil. If to some people is given great freedom, with it, they can commit a whole line of crimes.

I say, Love must come at its time. It has come already. Now the question is, what is the way from where the Love has come. In my view, in present day life, Love must begin from the fathers. So the Love must begin from above, from God and descend gradually into the families, into the father, the mother, the big brother, the big sister, until lastly it gets to the natural way. This way is the true way, upon which Love must go. This spring, this Love, which comes from God, you all must become conductors of, so it can come to all people. If we are open conductors for this Love, you will read all over the world its blessing. Then the hearts of all will open, and whatever we wish will come true. Everything in the world is in its place, however, the only thing is, when the rich work, they work without Love and when the poor rest, they rest without Love. When the professor gives his lectures, he teaches for money, not out of Love. When a doctor heals, he heals for money, not out of Love. When a priest serves he serves for money too, not out of Love. Today, Love is not a stimulus in the lives of people. Consequently, when you do one good deed, think about Love. Let It be the stimulus in your life. Yet, It still does not represent that true Love which must become the foundation of the present day life.

"Love your neighbor like yourself!"

5, p. 197

For now the influence of the moon is shown through sterling silver, but the sterling silver is one healing element. If we understood the properties of the moon, you would have been able to use sterling silver as an element for curing of many diseases. So sterling silver transforms the energies which come from the moon. Gold on the other hand transforms solar energy. This is the reason why people wear gold rings and jewelry, as well as precious stones. Especially when people get married, they wear gold rings and precious gems. The religious people say, man does not need any rings. No, even five rings to wear on a man's hands is good. You will say that it is superstitious for a man to think that if he wears gold rings they will be healing him. We consider this as superstition, but when we take some medication, we do not consider it; it is superstitious. You will take some kind of salt, some medication and you will think, that it will heal you. But the medication has been tested. I think the medication can heal inasmuch as is your trust in them. If you knew how to use water, you would have been able to heal yourself with it. There are people that have been chosen by Nature for doctors. Why? Inasmuch she has created them for the purpose to work for the restoration of man's normal condition. That is why, namely the doctors, have been sent by Nature.

5, p. 207

That which is tormenting people now is the question, which faith is the most right one? For me the right faith is the one which resurrects man; the right faith is that one, which enlightens man's mind; the right faith is that one, which ennobles man's heart; the right faith is that one, which improves life; the right faith is that one, that brings peace, joy and gladness among all people. This is faith.

5, p. 207

Life by itself on its own cannot be improved. In life, there is variety. There is not a single method through which life can be improved. You say, they, the methods, must be good, but remember one thing. There are many methods upon which man must work and with which he is working with presently. One method cannot be applied for two people. My trials have come to that. To be useful to each man, in order to rectify him, you have to apply one specific way, a method that applies for his uplifting. If you do not apply this method, he will become an ordinary man. If you apply on him one corresponding, specific method, this man will be uplifted. You will help for his upliftment. For this can be given some examples. All great people in the world owe their uplifting first to their mothers as inculcators of higher personal qualities and then to their fathers. So, behind himself, a man must have one great mother and one great father, but not one ambitious father and one ambitious mother. He must have such a mother and a father, who would say, whatever our son or daughter achieve, it is our achievement. This is the right life, because the good of one man is a good for the whole of humanity. The good of the whole of humanity is a good for the individual man as well. This idea must be laid in the new foundations of life. People are important and for themselves and for each other, as the leaves of one tree. In healthy trees the leaves do not fall down. In the healthy people the thought does not get lost.

5, p. 207

Every man in his life has the need for connection with the invisible world. I am talking about such a connection, that can make man free and noble. The issue is not just to believe in the other world, but the other world for the man must be like the clean air and the light, which he accepts in each moment. This air and this light will exert their influence upon him. When man gets connected with this world, he will notice how all of his talents are gradually developing in him and that he is already gradually coming out of the bodies of the ordinary man. He will be either gifted or genius. In this situation, whatever hardships are put before the talented, he neither gets dispirited, nor gets despaired. The genius, even if ten obstacles are put before him, he will overcome all of them. For him hardships do not exist. However, it is not like that for the ordinary man.

5, p. 211

With this I want to lead you to the law, when a man believes in something, he has a faith which is powerful, strong and with it creates miracles. All talented and genius people have had such a faith. Faith is a way for achievement. The nicest things in the world in all areas have happened by way of faith. In this case, as a force, faith can be applied in all areas of human life. It is not just for one man and one instance. It has different manifestations. There is something special in each man who has this faith. When faith in man is developed, it creates in him a good mood. Those who study bovarism, when they put a flat surface above the eyes, see the angle that is formed between the beam coming from the eyes of the man and that plate, has different sizes. In the one who has faith, this angle is at least 45 degrees and the ray from the eyes is always pointing up. Such a man never gets discouraged. You put a thousand difficulties upon him, he does not fail. However, for the one for whom the angle is smaller than 45 degrees, that's why he does not endure the difficulties. He gets easily dispirited.

I say, man must firstly strive to lift up his look and with this he will develop in himself that ability through which to use the powers of nature for his development. The human brain is one powerful and beautiful battery, in which are put all of his riches. If you understand the laws of your head, all diseases, sufferings, misfortunes and misunderstandings will disappear. Just by touching your head, you will find God. He has made your head and you must seek him. God has made the head the man's radio. If you do not understand yourself, how will you understand nature? Firstly, a man must understand himself and then nature. In a given instance nature is a condition for him, but God is a principle, which lives inside every man. However, not as is understood by ordinary people. God manifests Himself from the inside. The inner world is bigger than the outer. If God is a principle, then nature is only a condition. If we understand this inner principle, we will understand nature as a condition. Nature is reasonable, and God is among us, but we must enter between the two inner and outer poles.

5, p. 212

That which you wish on people, returns back to you. Now till the New Eve, when you meet your friends, wish them the best, without saying many extra words. Around ten words are enough. You can wish man many things: you can wish him good health; or to become learned man; or to become a poet; musician; or a paint artist; to become a prominent doctor; or a statesman and etc. . You can wish a man to get rich and not to be in any crisis.

5, p. 215

Correct your mind, so it can correct your body. Correct your heart, so it can correct your feelings. I wish good to all good people around the world. In my view he who makes mistakes is not bad. Somebody can err, he could have fallen, but in this man there is one grief, one sorrow and he is in torment, he is crying, he wants to live humanely. No matter how he is trampled by the other people, he has only one wish, to set himself right. Such a man is good. I say: "To all such people, who have fallen like that, but wish to set themselves right, give them help." I do not talk about those, who do not want to correct themselves. I do not talk about those wealthy, who do not think about anything. They are in their places. There are rich people in the world, who do not know what to do with their wealth. They do not know how to use it. They say: "Give us a plan to know how to use our wealth." Let there be in all of you be born one good wish to help with your good thoughts and feelings, with your good actions all good people, in whom there is a good wish to set themselves right, regardless of their faith, regardless of their social system, without any indifference. Be ready to help all. The good that you apply towards them, will return back to you.

5, p. 215

When you are at school, the professor will give you a lecture, one, two, three, four years in a row, but when you graduate the school, you will get out and you will have to show your abilities, you have to begin to give. To give from this which you have received. You will begin to give from yourself. What bad is there in this, to begin to give a small part of this what the teachers have given you?

5, p. 219

I say, the deep meaning of life lies in the understanding of Love, which gives an impulse to the human mind, the human heart and the human will for the greatest things, which man can do. You are sitting sometimes and say to yourself, "We want to be rich, to be learned, to be strong." You are not looking at life concretely. Each seed, that is planted in the ground, has all the potentialities in itself, but the outer nature presents all conditions through which these potentialities can be developed. If you think that all that you wish for can be given to you from the outside or that you can achieve from the outside, you are lying to yourself, you do not understand life, you are going in the wrong direction. Now you want from God talents. No, God has given you conditions from the outside and has put the talents in you.

5, p. 223

At the end they pierced Christ in the ribs. Until even today Christ still has this wound between His ribs and cannot get healed. Christ's wound is opened. Do you know what a rabbi has said about the different nations and for the Jews as well? This learned rabbi, after determining which nation what place it will take, for the Jews he has said, that they will take that pierced place between the ribs of Christ, so they fill it. The whole Jewish nation will enter in that hole, in that pierced place, so that Christ's wound is healed. When Israel turns to Christ and fills out that hole, then the whole of humanity will be set right.

Now the new understanding which you must have for the new year, insurmountable faith is required from all of you. Show at least partly this Divine Love, which acts in you.

5, p. 228

Love is concrete. In Love there is always one feeling, one desire to do a favor and to help. It does not make any difference between one being or another.

5, p. 228

Till you love one, but do not love the other one and until you differentiate between one man and another man, you have not understood the Will of God. It is a difficult thing to love man.

5, p. 231

Temptation inevitably will come. Temptation is a stumbling block in life, put there for the purpose of testing people.

5, p. 231

If suffering is in its place and is not a stumbling block in a man's life, it has a meaning. Suffering, which brings, after itself, knowledge for the soul, that suffering is in its place. A disease, which brings, after itself, strengthening of the body, that disease is in its place. Do not be afraid of diseases.

5, p. 233

In the Scripture it is said: "When God loves somebody, him He punishes, him He gives illnesses, him He gives sufferings, him He tests and to him He gives joy and merriment." So when you are suffering, God is treating you like a father. When you are in deprivations, God is testing you. If you are an ignorant man, rejoice that everyone is not an ignorant man; that there are learned people in the world, too. The contemporary scientists, who pass for such, are in the situation of the first adept, who say that they observed the Sun with their telescope. Yes, but the other one tells him: "I was there." The contemporary people are all learned, but the telescopes still remain. There are other scientists who have been on the Sun, and on Mars and on Venus and on Saturn and on Jupiter. For example Swedenborg has been on these planets and tells us what he saw.

5, p. 233

One Greek priest, I will not give an example with a Bulgarian priest, preached in the church the teaching of Christ and said, Christian brothers, Christ said that he who has two shirts should give one to the poor. As you can see, this teaching is a serious thing. After hearing this sermon, the priest's wife went home and began thinking about the Christ's words. At that time a beggar passed and stopped by their house to ask for something. Then the priest's wife said to herself, the priest has two shirts I'll give one to the beggar. She gave the shirt and was pleased that she fulfilled one of Christ's commandments. When the priest came back home from church, he started looking for something in his clothes and asked: Wife, where is my shirt? I gave it to a beggar who just passed by. You were saying that Christ said, that he who has two shirts should give one to the poor. Didn't' you? The priest responded, "This applies to other people, but not for us."

Contemporary people are seeking for one moral, which applies to other people, but not to themselves. So far it has been like that, but the right teaching firstly must affect us personally; we are to try it first on ourselves, and if it is right for us, it will be right for the others, too. After we give one shirt to our neighbor, we have to see how we will feel about it. Christ has said: "If you have two shirts, give one to your brother. "You say that this is the old teaching. What are you going to do with one shirt, when the time comes to wash your clothes? OK; you possess four shirts; so you give two to your brother, but two you leave for yourself. So if you have two shirts and you cannot give one to your brother, then increase the number of the shirts. If you have four shirts give two for the poor and two for yourself. If you have eight shirts, you should give four to the poor, and you will leave four for yourself. Consequently, if two shirts are too few for you then make them eight. This means, increase the good in you. Increase the power of your mind, increase the strength of your heart, increase the strength of your body.

5, p. 244

Like the bird which is raising her little ones. She goes all day long to gather food to feed them, but when they grow up, she lets them free to go to work. So, Love is that which does everything in the world. When you have Love, you can do anything. When you do not have Love, you can do nothing. The moral lies in the same. If we want to succeed in the world, we have to, by all means, have Love.

5, p. 248

God, Who loves us and Who has created us, has put everything good in us and wants from us to be representatives of the nice, the beautiful, which exist in the world. He can give us more than what we realize. In this meaning, everyone cannot only be a poet, but also a musician; not only a musician, but a painting artist; not only a painting artist, but a sculptor. Everyone can be a strong man. Man can be anything, no one can put a barrier in front of him. Then people are tripping over themselves when they divide themselves into men and women. The women say, we are from the gentle sex, we are not as strong as men. In my view, women operate with the most powerful force in the world. With Love. The mistake lies there, that the women have used

Love more for their own benefits, than for the benefits of their neighbors. Women have used Love more for their own temptation.

5, p. 248

Many ask, what did Christ teach? Christ taught that man's heart must be warm, but the man's mind must be cold. The man's soul must be filled with life, but the man's spirit must be filled with strength. Inasmuch, strength is a bearer of coldness in itself. He who is strong is cold. He who has life in himself has warmth.

5, p. 248

The trees must be kept with good care. In the future inculcation of high personal qualities, each man must have in his disposition five to ten trees for which he specifically has to care for. For the children's inculcation of high personal qualities this must be used as a method for them to care for the growing of specifically fruit trees. In this way the children can be re-educated in high personal qualities. Especially if the child is told that this pear or apple or plum tree is theirs and they must care for it: to water it, to grow it, to cultivate it. Now how are the children inculcated in high personal qualities? Their attention is not turned to the regular trees and the fruitful trees; and when they enter somebody else's garden, the first thing they do is climb up some plum tree or pear tree, shake it down and break its branches. The child does not have in mind that that the tree is reasonable. But when the child makes the fruitful trees grow, they will start loving them, they will get connected with them and will be inculcated with high personal qualities. You also need to know, that in you there are certain thoughts, which resemble the plants and you must grow them carefully. There are certain thoughts in the mental world, which are like the plants and we must plant them in our mind. There are also certain feelings, which are like the plants and these too we must plant in our heart. You want to inculcate yourself with high personal qualities, but you do not know how. If you cannot plant one thought in your mind and one feeling in your heart and to care for them like they were fruit trees, you will never be able to inculcate yourself with high personal qualities.

5, p. 265

The contemporary people have fallen into two opposite currents: some of them trust only in themselves, this is one of the extremes. The other ones trust only in God. The first and the second ones are wrong. To trust in God, this means to be outside of Him, this is an extreme. To trust in yourself, this is the other extreme. Both of the methods are incorrect. You are not a master of the whole world, how can you trust only in yourself? Man, in part, can trust in himself, but in part he can trust in God. Here is what I understand in the words: "Trust only in God." It means to expect from God to come and plow your field, to plant it with seeds, to bring you an Earthen jug of water, to study for you, to finish university for you and so forth. You say: "May God help us to become millionaires." Nature does not deal with that. There are things with which Nature deals with, but they are essential things. You ask: "Where is God?" God is in the light. When you learn the laws of the light, you are already entering in contact with God.

God is in the air. When you learn the law of the air, you will enter into contact with God. God is in the water. When you learn the law of the water, you will enter into contact with God. God is in the food. When you learn the law of the food, you will enter into contact with God. Consequently, man has four points of contact with God, through the light, through the air, through the water and through the food. Somebody comes to me, stands up proudly and asks: "Where is the Lord?" In the light. In the air. You do not know what is the air, you do not know the properties of the air. When this air enters your lungs and purifies the blood, gives an impulse to life, this namely is God. When you accept in yourself that property of the light, that gives you an urge for knowledge, this is God. When you accept in you that property of the water, which quenches your thirst, this is God. That property of the food, which gives strength, which gives health in man and maintains for eternity the stock of his strength, this is God.

5, p. 266

He who is in camaraderie with Love and Wisdom will always remain undefeated. This is because he has in himself the greatest warmth and light. With these no one can cause him harm. Do you know what kind of warmth is that? From that warmth the devil's hairs stand up. There is no unclean air, which, when falling into the fire of Love not to melt down, it melts down like a candle. When the devil sees the man of Love, the devil too runs away from him. And the bear runs away from this fire. Why? Hence when the bear comes close to it, it gets burned down. Love is the strongest fire. Wherever it passes, it melts down everything. Become a friend with

Love to see how all of your enemies will run away. All enemies disappear before the man of Love and only his friends remain. Only enemies run away from Love.

5, p. 266

I say, every man represents one number, either happy or unhappy. He who understands that great Divine law, he will avoid all those people who represent some unhappy number. It is not the issue for a man to avoid them, but not to meet them often. He will bypass him, will take another route so as not to meet him. If you want to acquire something, meet a happy man. He definitely will give you something from himself.

5, p. 278

Do you know what it means to understand one man? To understand one man means, in a given situation to make the same sacrifice for him as you would do for yourself. Not to hesitate even for a moment, without having two morals in yourself. To love one man means to be ready to sacrifice yourself for him as you would for yourself. Otherwise without this readiness for sacrifice, whatever you tell him, whatever moral situations you present him, they are empty words.

5, p. 280

The only thing that man will take with himself into the other world are those nicest minutes of his life, when he made those little good deeds which no one saw him doing. Only with those little good deeds will he enter into the invisible world. For all those good deeds which people saw him do, he has been paid already, there is nothing more he can expect for these seen deeds. For those good deeds for which the newspapers wrote, he has been paid his salary while on Earth. Only with the little good deeds, which no one saw will he enter into God's Kingdom. With these little good deeds you will enter, with them as an adornment, as your virtues, God's Kingdom. This means that you enter into the other world with your faith.

5, p. 281

To be a singer in the world, that is more than to be a king. On Earth you can be a king, but when you go to heaven, they prefer that you be a singer rather than a king. Why? Accordingly they already have there one king, but do not have enough singers. Consequently, I prefer to be a singer on Earth than a king. To a singer everybody will thank for giving them joy, but how many will thank a king? The king might have signed one or more death sentences, but the singer did not condemn anybody. The king might have forgiven somebody, not to be sentenced to death, but will give him a life sentence. The singer does not sue anybody. When the singer sings, he tells the people, enjoy your life, enjoy it, life is for you with all of its opportunities for achievements.

5, p. 282

Sometimes you think that when you sing, there is no one that is listening to you. They are listening from the invisible world. People are amazing with their wishes. They say, where is the invisible world? That's amazing! When the blind man is told that he lives in one visible world, he is wondering how he cannot see! How is it that he cannot see this visible world? Although he does not see it, he lives in the visible world. If his eyes get opened, he will see where this world is. He is not far away from it, it is around him. From my knowledge, the distance, the thickness, from this and the other world is only one hundred millionth of a millimeter of distance.

5, p. 282

It is good to keep your mouth clean. That means, never to allow impure vibrations to come out of your mouth. Imagine what would it mean to tell somebody, that you hate him, that you do not want to see him, that you do not have trust in him. Do not dirty your tongue with the remnants of the past generation! Say to yourself, I will live, I will study, God's powers to acquire. I will love all people on the face of the Earth, I will do whatever God wants, I will do good and so on. When somebody comes to visit you and stays for a few days in your home, do not look forward that he leaves, but tell him, "I am very pleased with your visit, since you came I began to pray and to work."

5, p. 282

There is one law, like attracts like! If we go by the law of harmony, in the great Divine world, around us there will always be attracted good people. In this world a thief cannot enter.

5, p. 287

You understand the future life so much, as much as the grasshopper has an idea about the human life. I have watched these grasshoppers, which I call "the happy musicians." When I sometimes come close to the hole of these musicians, with respect he right away moves back and says, "Welcome!" He cannot put himself in my position, he does not understand me. When I move away, he again shows up his head and begins to take a sunbath. Enormous is the difference in the lives and understandings of all beings! So you sometimes think that the angel is like the man. Tremendous is the difference between the lives of angels and the lives of men. The life of one angel is more real, than the lives of entire mankind. Here is what to read in it. The biography of an angel is much more interesting, than that of all mankind. There are a lot of interesting things in it. An angel has gone through many things, until he arrived to that situation. There are things for a man to read, to get inspired.

5, p. 288

Here is what I understand in the words natural food. The natural food for each organism is that one, which has the same vibration as the human organism itself. Each food, that does not have the same vibrations as your organism, do not eat it, it is not for you, nothing more! This food is harmful to you. Hygienic food is that which has the same degree of vibrations as your organism.

5, p. 294

According to the understanding of present day people, the rich pass as a smart man, but the poor, even being smart, again passes as a fool. No, man's wealth does not determine the quality of his mind. Wealth is a result of human activity. A smart man is he who does not create for himself unnecessary sufferings. Every man, who creates sufferings for himself, his intellect is not a strong one. He has mediocre intellect.

5, p. 298

The reason for the disagreement among the nations is, that each nation wants to take first place, to be the first among the nations on Earth, but this is not in the order of things. God has chosen one nation in the world, but this nation is neither the English, nor the Jewish, nor any other nation as we know them. This nation is the whole of humanity. This God chosen nation is comprised of all beings, of all people who think. Man is distinguished namely by his thought. By that I define man. At the same time I say, this man who rectifies his mistakes, he is a man. He who does not rectify his mistakes, he is an animal. Think whatever you want, that's how I understand it. The animal is distinguished by this, that it cannot rectify its mistakes. That is why the wolf, for thousands of years, will still be a wolf. Boil him, bake him, the wolf will remain a wolf. Even if he finishes four faculties, he will still remain a wolf. The same thing I can say about the bear. Boil her, bake her, she will remain a bear. Even if she finishes four faculties, she will still be a bear. The boa, no matter what it is told, it will still be a boa. An animal is an animal. Whereas that thinking being, which is created by the image and likeness of God, which can rectify his mistakes and which progresses, that is man. As he works consciously upon himself, he can change one condition with another. Man can rectify not only his mistakes, but also the mistakes of other people around himself. Then man's life will be understood for himself and it will acquire a different meaning.

5, p. 298

Each person, whose head on top is concave (curved inward), shows that he lacks something. You do not look at what a man is outside, what is his automobile. For me, it is not important if a man outside is white or reddish or blue, this is not important. For me it is important what a man is in geometrical terms. What are the lines on him, straight or curved. For me it is also important the mathematical forces, which have worked upon him. Nature works by some mathematical and geometrical laws. She has put all things in man in a strictly defined way. For example, she has put the mouth correctly, according to the love that acts in him. In the nose, she has put his intelligence. The reasonableness she has put in his ears. Strength she has put in his hands. The virtues she has put in his legs and the good she has put in his stomach. The decrees and his inner economical conditions she has put in his lungs and the whole state apparatus she has put in the brain. This is one whole world which man must study.

5, p. 301

For me it is important what you can do. Stop at that, that is given to you and what you can do at the given moment. There is one law, which has been checked out for thousands of years up to now. This law is the following: "Never allow one negative thought to gain the upper hand in your consciousness. In no way allow such a thought." Somebody comes to you and says: "Do you know that your father died?" Leave this thought aside. Another comes and says: Do you know that such and such bank failed? Put that thought aside! Another one comes and says: "Do you know that you are fired?" Leave this thought aside! If you are truly fired, you must know that you are in one human order. That means, people have hired you as a teacher and they will fire you as a teacher. They have appointed you as a manager and they will fire you as a manager. Or, they have appointed you as a minister and they will fire you as a minister. However, this for which nature has put you, from there no one can fire you. Even if the whole world gathers to fire you, no one can fire you. No one can fire a man from that job, for which nature has appointed him. This must enter as a rule, as a law in our life. In this case you will be the master of your situation. Then what is left for you? Only to do the Will of God.

5, p. 301

The truth cannot be old. If the truth is old, that means it has changed. The truth can be neither old or young. It can neither grow old, nor get younger. The truth is that beginning, which gives the eternal process of development and which gives meaning to life. The whole world sits in the truth, there is no any other meaning behind the truth. The only thing that makes people's ultimate life meaningful, is the truth. When we are glad and merry, this is the truth in us that has caused this joy. When man achieves something in the world, he is in the world of truth. All human achievements are due to the truth. If a man loves the truth, it will always help him.

5, p. 305

The Divine Spirit, which comes upon you, you do not expect to see It. That impulse, that thought, that feeling, which enters you and make you work, that is the Divine. No matter how weak, no matter how small that thing is, pay attention to it, because from it you will receive the biggest blessing and the biggest good.

5, p. 305

Mishap, this is the human order. These mishaps, the sufferings in the world are allowed, so we get out of the human order and enter the Divine, i.e. in the order of nature. The human order of things is necessary, you cannot avoid going through it. So, in order to enter the Divine order, we have to firstly go through the human, through the transient world.

5, p. 309

The outer conditions, these are the Divine conditions, the environment, in which people live. Those people, with which you are surrounded, they are purposely put there by God for your education. Whatever your understanding may be, this is important for you to know. All of you will not live in one and the same environment.

5, p. 313

So, after thousands and millions of years, the Earth and the Sun will be in a completely different place in space from the one they are occupying now. This is a philosophical system which only the great people can understand. Consequently, for you, every single man is their own small world. That's why each man with whom you are in contact with, you should know, that he is necessary for your upliftment. This is as if you understand him; if you do not, he will become the cause for your downfall. Remember that! Each man with whom you are in contact and you understand him, you will be uplifted; if you do not understand him, you yourself will become the reason for your fall and get hurt. Believe in everything in the world and in the good and in the evil is God! Thus is by principle. If you understand God, He manifests Himself as good in you. If you do not understand Him, He manifests Himself as evil in you. When you repent, He stops tormenting you. When you are stubborn, He punishes you. Why is it like that? So far no one has given an explanation. You must know one thing, everything is inside God! Evil is created by us, because we want to act upon the Lord, to make Him think like us. No, that is impossible. It is impossible for you to make the Lord to think like us. If we fulfill the Divine plan, which is set out for us for our development, we will become greater people than we can ever imagine. In this and in your future life, you will always have good conditions. I say, do not think about the future, think for today. If you have however bitter thoughts, bitter feelings and desires, all of that, throw it out! Leave only the pure ones and begin creative work upon yourself! What other people have achieved, put that aside. What you will achieve, this is important to you. The achievement of other people is an achievement for us as well. The achievement of the whole of humanity one day will be an achievement for us as well.

5, p. 313

So thought is necessary, because without it no transformation in the world can occur. The thought is the first impulse of the soul. If you do not think right, you must know, that whatever work you begin, be it religious, be it scientific or trade related, you will not succeed. If you do not think right, there will always come on you some catastrophe, there will always be something wrong that happens to you. If you think right, all catastrophes will be avoided. If you think right, again tests will still come upon you, but those tests will be musical, they will be properly distributed.

5, p. 317

"**I** am the living bread, which came down from heaven and whoever eats me, he will acquire the eternal life." *(John 6: 51)* Many asked themselves is that possible? How is it possible to eat man? Some of His disciples left Him, they could not understand this thing. They said to themselves, there is something strange here. This thing is not scientific. Christ had in mind the reasonable word and that is why He was saying: "I am the word." He spoke about the reasonable word. So, there is a word, which brings the bread with itself. Consequently, if you find that word you will never be in need.

Now, do not have any illusions to think that things can be easily done.

5, p. 319

Man, to whom the spirit talks to, he does not think about himself and he always takes the last place. He is for the improvement of the lives of all people. His life is set right, there is nothing that needs to be set right. When the lives of others are set right, then his life is set right. Should the hand think how to set right its life? The setting of the life of the hand right depends on the setting of the life of the body right. The setting of the life of the body right depends on the setting of the life of the head right, and so on.

5, p. 323

I say, that Love, which connects people in one and puts them in the situation to understand each other and to work together, this is the Divine Love, the Love in which everyone is ready to do for the other one such sacrifices, as he is ready to do for himself. This is the true Love! This is the Divine Love, but with the human love, each one marries for personal benefits.

5, p. 325

I say, this order of things is temporary. Firstly, we have to know that we are sent on Earth to learn how to think. The first thing is, man must acquire the right thought, because everything else, which man will acquire, is determined by the right thought. Not that life is bad, but without the right thought, the road along which we walk will bring us a whole line of misfortunes.

5, p. 325

All people must be smart be able to think right. This is the solution of the difficult issue in life. Without the right thought, human nature cannot be known. I often talk about Love, but Love is not this, which people think is Love. In my view the happy life emerges from Love, but Love does not live in life, it is outside of life. Love is not in the reasonable life, it is manifested through a reasonable life. It is outside the reasonable life. Love is one great power in the world. When it comes, it only gives and leaves. Such, it is said, in a human way. It will never join up with you. When it comes to you, it will put something in your hand and will leave. It is a power with which nothing is restricted. Sometimes you want to have Love in you. No, make use of the benefits of Love, without wanting to keep it for yourself. This is life. Make use of Love. It lasts only a moment, which cannot be preserved. When this moment comes, you will never forget it. What a thing is Love's visit I will liken it with the following story: Once upon a time one shepherd did a favor to an old-time king. A beast attacked the king, and the shepherd saved him from that beast. By some other circumstance this shepherd was sentenced to death. When the verdict was taken to the king for signing, the king said, stop this verdict and let the shepherd go free. You cannot convict this man, because he saved my life. The king gave him a hug, kissed him and took him to his palace, fed him and let him go to his herd. Thus, he freed him from the gallows. Such thing is Love. It frees him from the gallows and sends him to go to his herd. When Love comes, it will free you from all of your difficulties in your life and will send you to your people. Now the other things, that we have in life, they are right too, but are all temporary. Now, heroes are wanted in the world.

5, p. 327

Christ says: "I am the living bread."*(John 6: 51)* But this bread cannot be eaten without Love. That is one rule. You cannot eat the living bread if you do not have Love in you. If you do not have Love, it cannot be caught; the living bread is elusive.

5, p. 329

I do not talk about this love that you know, but for the Love which is coming now into the world. It is coming to help us. It is that moment, that impulse for the Good, which will put us in the right direction. For this Love I am talking about, not from the outside, but from the inside. A great moment is this moment of Love!

This is the living bread which you must eat with love. If you cannot love your mother, your father, your brothers and sisters, then I do not know who can help you. Who can you love then? If you cannot love your teachers, your servants, who are helping you, then I do not know who can help you! Firstly, love those who have been loyal and who have served you, and then you will take the second step, you will turn to those who have done you mischief. This is the last work yet, this is about your enemies. Firstly, find those who have been loyal to you, be grateful to them and afterwards (show love) to your enemies.

This is the living bread, which has come down from above to improve the world. This is how you all have to be thinking. The world by itself afterwards will get arranged right.

5, p. 329

For example, Moses has said: "An eye for an eye." *(Exodus 21: 24)* However, Christ said: "If they hit you on the cheek, offer them the other also." *(Luke 6: 29)* How will you reconcile these contradictions? In addition to that, Christ has said: "If someone takes your coat, give him the under shirt also." *(Luke 6: 29)* Somewhere else, He said: "Do not retaliate against your enemies, but love them." *(Matthew 5: 39)* I ask: How will you reconcile all these contradictions? Which one is right? Each one, who has spoken at his time is right. Moses spoke to the Jews in accordance of the then Jewish understandings. He spoke to the children, nothing more. However, Christ spoke to the older ones, and He spoke to them with parables.

5, p. 331

What is, for example, theft? Or what is a lie? A lie is one result. It is one action. A lie goes by the female line. She is not a boy, but a girl, a young girl around 12 years old and is sly and cunning such that she can twine and confuse anyone's head. This is already a figure of speech. Here is what I understand when I say that a lie goes by the female line. In a lie the salt is predominant over the acid. Consequently, when dominance is given to the acid in man, a lie is born. When the acids are predominant over the alkalines, bravery is born.

Consequently, in brave people the acids are predominant. Someone among you may say, that this is not clear to them. What should I do if it is not clear to them? You will say to explain it. I cannot explain it to you. There are things which cannot be explained, they must be done.

5, p. 333

What can human thought do? Human thought must reduce, to a certain degree, the human stomach. With the contemporary development of people the stomach has a predominance. The stomach represents the salts, the lungs represent the alkaline, but the brain represent the acids. Consequently, we have more salts than we need. Salts always cause constipation. Constipation in the body is due to certain salts. I do not know what the contemporary doctors think about this issue, but my diagnosis, according to the new teaching, shows that constipation is due to the salts in the body. The abundance of alkaline causes an abundance of venous blood, but the abundance of the acids in the brain causes neurasthenia. When acids dominate in the brain of a man, he definitely will be neurasthenic. When alkaline is dominant in the breathing system of a man, he definitely will have an abundant amount of venous blood. When the salts are dominant in the human body, then the stomach will dominate and as a consequence obesity will appear and from there different diseases as well.

Consequently, man must have one good organism. I am talking about those acids in life, which are governed by the human reasonableness. I am talking about those alkalines, which are governed by the human reasonableness. I am talking about those salts, which are governed by the human reasonableness. There are salts that are in their place, but there must be no surpluses in the human body.

5, p. 340

Christ gives an example of a rich man, who had a lot of wheat, who filled his barns and said to his soul, now you will have a lot to eat and to drink. I'll be glad and I'll be merry. *(Luke 12: 13 - 21)* But God said to him, you fool, this evening I will take your soul. To whom will you leave all that wheat? Do not think that if you have money in the bank you are secured. Your life is short. You must not trust only in your money. If you have 100 million leva (BG currency), they can be like one lev. You must not get discouraged. Without having a nickel, be again rich, you must feel above the conditions. Even having a hundred million leva, you again feel like you have nothing. With both situations you must not forget yourself. The reasonable man disposes with everything that is out there in nature. You cannot put your trust in the banks. The banks are not made by reasonable people. The banks are only one educational tool to teach people certain things. This system, in which we live, is created for children for the purpose to teach the children higher personal qualities. It is an excellent system, but it is not for the saints.

5, p. 341

I ask, what was Christ's intimate thought, when He told His disciples to be as wise as snakes and as harmless as doves? *(Matthew 10: 16)* With that, Christ wanted to say, that the snake is the acid, the alkaline is the pigeon, but you are the result, the salt. Be reasonable as the snakes and have the acid of the snakes. Have the alkaline of the doves, so you can give the result, the salt. If you cannot understand the acid, the snake is like an acid in you and the dove as an alkaline in you, they will produce opposite results in you. The snake, with its acid, will create poison in your body and it will poison you. If you do not understand the qualities of the alkaline in you, you will create for yourself other difficulties. If you acquire the qualities of the dove and become perfectly soft, you will have no bravery in you, you will become very fearful. Many of the contemporary good people are fearful. They are good because of the fear, but not from convictions. Somebody is good and looks like he follows the law. When he looks to fulfill the law out of fear, this man is only one third good. If the law forces you to be good, you are good by only one third. You are good, but by only one third.

5, p. 342

If I quote you the verse of Christ: "Be reasonable." *(1 Thessalonians 5: 19 - 21)* here is what my idea is. The bad conditions you are in, I consider a prison. Since you are now in prison, one day, when you get out of this prison, remember my words, be as reasonable as the snakes and as harmless as the dove, so you do not find yourself in prison again.

Now you have to endure the sufferings. Not that I want you to suffer, but I say, that you have to endure the sufferings.

5, p. 342

The way of sufferings is the way of Moses' law. Until we go through Moses' law, through the law of suffering, we cannot come to Christ's law. The whole political life, the whole social system, is all the law of Moses. We have to pass through the whole social system. When we learn all things, they by themselves will become meaningless to us, for the future generation. That is why you shall leave aside the questions regarding the present day system. That is how the great law is.

5, p. 343

So, now each one of you must make inner experiments. This is necessary, so he boosts his strength. Man's strength is acquired from his thoughts and wishes. You must know this! You cannot be strong, you cannot overcome the difficulties of your life, if you are not pure by thought and feelings. Afterwards the strength will come. So now it is necessary for the good people in the world to carry the best and the purest possible thoughts!

5, p. 344

So the practical life requires the following: do not be sorry for your present life; do not be sorry for your present mistakes; do not be sorry for your present thoughts, feelings, actions; do not be sorry for anything; only set yourself straight! Use everything, that is given to you, because that, which you think and feel, is not only yours; it belongs to the whole of humanity.

5, p. 345

Therefore be reasonable! Reasonableness lies in this, to live right.

5, p. 345

So the first thing, become masters of your thoughts, not all at once, but gradually. Become masters of your feelings, not all at once, but gradually. Do not be sorry for anything, but constantly make one small effort. No matter how microscopic that effort is, do not get discouraged. You may have thousands of slippings a day, that should not worry you. Do not be sorry for anything, because this, what you wanted to achieve, but you could not, others have achieved it. One day, you will possess what others have already achieved. One day, as a musician, you will take part in what others have achieved. Since today almost the whole of humanity takes part in music and one day you will benefit from their achievements. You can benefit from your reasonableness too, and one day you will benefit from the reasonableness in the whole of humanity. You do only what is your duty, but the other things you leave to God, let God arrange the other things!

5, p. 346

In the word God, I understand to be the only being, which neither changes, nor alters. He is a being which is limitless, without having any limits. God is a Being which has, in His disposition, all things and does things in such a way, as He deems them to be good. Consequently, behind Him, there is no other being. For Him there is no law. He Himself is the law. Be always in agreement with Him and you will see how your life will change and will be set right. If people understood today this great law, their life would be changed in an instant.

5, p. 346

The world cannot have a correct understanding unless Love has preceded the understanding. Love lies before and higher than any understanding. Love precedes the reasonableness. Reasonableness is the result of the great in life, the Love. When it is said, that God is Love, *(1 John 4: 8)* it must be known that it is Love that arranges all things in the world. Everything in the world emerges from Love which we do not realize; consequently, we want to arrange our life outside of Love. This is impossible! If our mothers had not sacrificed themselves for our sake, if our brothers and sisters had not sacrificed themselves for our sake, if the plants and the animals would not have sacrificed themselves for our sake, what would have happened to us? Everywhere, we see only sacrifices and we see that this Love does not regret for sacrifices made, not even a single bit. It is a pleasure for Love that it has made these sacrifices, but since we do not understand the law, the law of Love, we suffer. I consider that the sufferings are the result of not understanding the law of Love. If you do not understand the sufferings, understand at least the law of Love, then the sufferings will come to their natural position. Imagine, that in the world there are beings who do not have any sufferings; there are beings who make no mistakes at all, who never think wrong at all. Their thoughts are always pure and right. These beings live thanks to their pure thoughts and wishes. You say that the whole world is wicked. Not all people are like you sinners, they are not at your level, they do not have your views. We do not do what the animals do, we do something more than what they do. Consequently, in man there is one good trait, he wants to study, he wants to be a candidate to be a disciple of the school of Love! Now I want you all to enter this school of Love. Then, only your adversities and hardships will gradually be arranged. There, in the school, you will learn everything! Outside of this school all things are vacillating, there is no solution of the issue. You may theoretically know something, but you cannot have an inner understanding of the discontent. When you enter this school, an inner transformation will happen in you and you will see that life can be different and that one can live differently. Now, for the time being, this is impossible, but when you enter the school of Love, then everything will be arranged and everything can be achieved.

Therefore be reasonable, in order for you to enter the school of Love!

5, p. 346

Christ asks: "By what, are distinguished the good people?" The good people are distinguished by this, that they produce good fruits. The good fruit, this is the real in the world. The bad fruit is the transient in the world. In this situation there cannot be an exchange between good and evil. Good and evil are incompatible for the sole reason that good belongs to one eternal order, but evil belongs to one temporary order. On this foundation there cannot be an exchange between good and evil. Their values are different; because, you cannot replace the value of one eternal fruit with something, which tomorrow will completely lose its value.

Man is something more than what he knows and understands about himself. All people, who make experiments and observations in the field of the magnetism, but not hypnotism, have noticed particular manifestations in man, when he is put in a magnetic sleep from the third stage upward. I am not talking about hypnotism as if it was one specific process, but I have in mind the magnetism. If a man is put in a magnetic sleep of the first, second or third level, he will find himself in the situation of illusions, they are the areas of illusions. They can tell a man that there is water around him, which he must swim through or that there is a wall which he cannot cross over, they will be laughing around him, but he will be trying to swim through the water, or he will stop before the wall which does not exist at all. However, if he goes from the third level of magnetic sleep upward, into the fourth or fifth level, he already becomes a master of himself and no one can give him commands. Up to the third level the others can be his masters and manage him, but when he passes the fifth level, he is no longer giving into any magnetizing. In this situation, this man, who has not studied anywhere, does not know any medicine, but can show himself off as a most experienced doctor. It is only enough to present him with a patient and he will most successfully determine the patient's diagnosis. He will say that this man is infected with tuberculosis of the left side and down and will prescribe him medication, which will be very effective. When he wakes up from this sleep, this man will be again the same, whatever he was before the sleep. I ask, how can you explain this situation? Why this is so, is another matter, however, the experiments made in this direction show that in man there are abilities and knowledge that in a given case can eventually be awoken and fall asleep again. I say, the bad conditions in which contemporary people are being placed and about which they complain, are not the bad conditions. These are opportunities for the development of the higher human abilities. So, every hardship that a man has is nothing else, except an opportunity to develop his sublime abilities, to awaken in him something more than what he usually shows. The greater the hardships and the sufferings are for man, the greater the abilities that are being developed in him, the greater the abilities that awaken in him, for his development. If that was not so, then the sufferings and the limitations would have been without any meaning. If it is a matter for us just to suffer, each suffering in man is compensated with this, that in him is developed one inner ability, one sense, from which depends his own good. Whoever cannot make use of the suffering, then in him is born the philosophy, to have the ability to free himself of the sufferings as soon as possible. You all can free yourself from the sufferings. When? When you do not wear tight shoes and when your pockets are filled with gold. You can all free yourself from the suffering, but when? When your heads are full with knowledge, and with it you understand the laws of nature, when you are a genius paint artist, so that wherever you go, you can paint any piece of art work or a picture. You can all free yourself from the suffering, when you are excellent musicians and to know how to pull the bow or to play the piano and wherever you go you can play music right away.

5, p. 373

The real is distinguished by the transient. Whether you are in reality or in the transient is known by two things. Until you are disturbed you are in the transient world. When in your soul, sets in that self-confidence, that quiet peace, and you realize, that nothing in the world is by accident, but is directed by one great reasonableness. Then you are in the world of the real. A Bulgarian officer told me of one of his personal experiences, which happened during the war, which he cannot explain to himself to this day: "One day the regimental commander sent to me a Bulgarian soldier with an order, while at the same time the Serbs were shooting with their machine guns, rifles and their artillery. This soldier had to go through this fire, but he walked quietly and calmly. When I saw him coming, I said to myself, "They will kill this man. Whatever order the regimental commander gave him, he'll be hardly able to pass through. Couldn't he find another way, but he had to send this man through the fire." I too gave my order to the soldier, who had to return back. The soldier accepted the order and went calmly back. Not even a single bullet touched him. Up to this day I cannot explain to myself how this happened. I say, there is something reasonable which directs the faith of people. There are people who cannot die, this the Indians (from India) call a dead zone, in which the fire does not act. They also call it the law of exceptions. All reasonable people are required to study the laws of nature. This shows that there is one common Providence of God. Do not consider that this Providence is something mechanical. According to this common

Providence, every man has his own place and purpose to function as one organ, as one cell, in a given place and in given conditions. Until you are in the specified place in your body, you are secure. If you get out of your body then your freedom is being limited. Man's finger is free until it stays in the body, man's leg is free, until it stays in the body. Man by himself is a part of one larger organism. The Scripture says: "We are all parts of one common organism." *(Romans 12: 4)* Consequently, no one lives for himself only. The big mistake in the world is due to this, that we think and wish each one to secure his own life.

5, p. 375

There is one instance in which man must secure himself, and this is the knowledge which man must acquire. In that, lies all the insurance. To solve the difficulties, to solve the causes of the contemporary difficulties which are in our individual lives, in our family life, in our social and state life, as well as the difficulties that arise in the whole of humanity. There are reasons for all of this. We are not sent on Earth to solve the hardships of the whole of humanity, because the purpose of those hardships is completely different.

5, p. 376

"If you are not born anew, you cannot enter the Kingdom of God."*(John 3: 3)* Anew means, that you are born from water and spirit. In other words, if you are not ready to leave the swine (in ref. to the son who had to eat pods with the swine to survive), if you are not ready to repent for all of your foolishness, that you have eaten everything from your father and have lived wastefully you cannot enter into the new conditions, you cannot be born from water and spirit. You will say: "Why is all that necessary?" If you are not born anew, if you do not repent, you will die together with the swine, nothing more. You can have an objection against me, that so many people are being honored, that monuments have been built for them. I feel sorry for all the people who have monuments of themselves. I wish to never have a monument of myself.

5, p. 387

For me death is a torn cloth. When a man dies, this shows that his cloth is torn and he is given a new cloth. So, the clothes die, but not the man. Man never dies. Man's torn clothes are put to the side, but man himself never dies. The clothes at times are born, at times die. This idea may not be clear to you, but it is okay.

5, p. 387

If sometimes there is no doctor, in your disposition, you can call some poor musician to play you some music, but in his music there should be no flats. Let him play major scales and to often repeat some tones. Whatever disease you may have, if you sing or play music for around half an hour, your illness definitely will go way. Music has the ability to change the vibrations of the body. Each illness shows that in man there is some musical lowering. He is below the level of the music. The sick are not in a disposition to sing. If the sick do not sing, they are condemned to death. If the sick are inclined to sing, they have conditions to restore their health. There is one statistic about that. Surely, if you kill, in man, the desire to sing, you are condemning him to death; in him occurs degradation. Life by itself is nothing else, but one musical exhibition of the Divine life. Life by itself is a musical rhythm. While we keep that musical rhythm, we live. When we lose that rhythm, into us come all diseases. In this case we have to recommend music. The music is an introduction for that Divine tempo of the music. From that music there is one higher level. So when some disease comes into you, sing, hum to yourself. Sing the tone "do" 50 times. If you are anemic, lazy or indolent, sing the tone "re" 99 times. If you do not like to think, sing the tone "mi" 80 times. If you are a little bit absentminded, wasteful and you do not like the material things, sing the tone "fa" 75 times. If you do not like justice sing the tone "sol" 101 times. If you do not like the arts and painting art, sing the tone "la" 110 times. If you are not religious and you are not believers in God, but you want to become such, sing the tone "si" (in Bulgarian) = "ti" 150 times. This is a theory, it is easy to say. There is a school, in which man studies how to combine these tones. There is one combination of these tones. Firstly, they will be sung in takts. It must be known what the intervals between the tones will be. Then, it must be known whether whole tones will be sung, or half, or one fourth, one eight etc.

5, p. 388

If you basically always use music, you will have the opportunity to cure yourself probably 75 out of 100 times, more than now, when you are not in a musical disposition. Therefore, see to it that you have an optimistic disposition.

Optimism is due to the music. The present day music is a blessing for the world. I would wish for the future that each home plays a musical instrument. Each one must be able to play on some musical instrument, be it a guitar, a mandolin, a violin, a citrus, a shepherd's pipe or at last a bagpipe; but each one must be able to play on some instrument. If there are no instruments, you can use 10 dishes and rattle them. So now the scientific conclusion. We are now in the world and we have to have a clear idea about it.

5, p. 389

Happiness is something great. When a man arrives at happiness, he must be very smart. For a man to be happy, he must be something more than a saint. The saint too cannot be completely happy. Happiness exists only in one condition. Happiness is the result of Divine Love. He who lives in this Love, he can only be happy.

5, p. 390

Everyone thinks that he can become a statesman, to rule over the world. That's why everyone says: "If I can only become once a prime minister, I will hang all those who disobey my orders." This is the secondary rule, the rule through violence. No, the world cannot be ruled like that. The world cannot be set right in this way. Those who do not understand say: "Wooden stick for these people, there is no need to talk to them. Drub him as necessary, and he will keep quiet." For a man to be a statesman, he must be the most learned man in the world. He must understand in depth human nature, the human soul, the human mind, the human heart, he must understand from out of the depth the human powers, to take into account all things.

5, p. 390

For the poor to get rid of their poverty, they must love working and be patient. In this lies their salvation. For the rich to keep their wealth, they must be generous and pure. Who can be pure? Only the honest and just can be pure. That is how I interpret purity. In my view, purity is a symbol, an emblem of justice and honesty. That is how this issue lies in my mind. The generous man is the man of Love. You cannot be generous, if Love has not permeated into your soul. If you are rich and you want to keep your wealth, you must love all people around you, you must be honest and just. Thus all people around you will cooperate with you and thus you will form one family.

5, p. 392

Love is an image of God accessible to us. This image is understandable to our soul and our heart. The image of wisdom, of knowledge is understandable for our mind and for our intelligence. The image of Truth and freedom is accessible for our will and for our reasonableness in the world. Consequently, in the world there are three Divine forms with which, in the given situation, we can work with: the heart, the mind and the will. With the heart we have to work with those forces, with those forms, with which the Divine Love works. With our mind we have to work with those forms, with those forces, with which the Divine Wisdom works. Lastly, through our reasonableness or through our will, through the highest in us, we have to work with those forms, with those forces, with which the Truth works, with which freedom works.

5, p. 393

It is often said that life without sufferings cannot be understood. Yes, but there are sufferings that are sweet, but there are some that are bitter. The bitter sufferings poison life, but the sweet sufferings prolong life. There are some torments that are sweet and there are some torments that poison man, which destroy him. I make this distinction; I ask, which torments and sufferings do you have, the sweet or the bitter ones? If you have the bitter ones, try to free yourself from them as soon as possible. If they are the sweet ones, look that their fruits ripen sooner. Each man must have something to lean on.

5, p. 403

For his happiness, man must love working. For his happiness, man must be generous. Man must be pure for his happiness. That is the way for him to unite the qualities of the poor and the qualities of the rich into one, so he can be happy. Wealth and poverty are two opposing poles of happiness. Man can never be happy if he has not been through the school of poverty and through the school of wealth. Only in this situation can man be happy. Consequently, poverty and wealth are two schools for you so you can enter into the area of life, which bears happiness.

5, p. 394

All people are rich by mind and by heart, but they do not use their riches. With his mind and with his heart, man can ruin his happiness. With a single word you can close your way and with a single word you can open your way. With a single look you can open your way and with a single look you can close your way. Do you know that if you say one word to somebody out of place, he won't be able to forget it, even in twenty years. I ask, how will we inculcate higher personal qualities in ourselves, how will people inculcate higher personal qualities in themselves? Firstly, the human heart must be freed from all unnecessary human wishes. Secondly, the human mind must be freed from all unnecessary human thoughts. Then man must be left to function with only those Divine thoughts and wishes with which he was born, but not with those which were thrust upon the man, afterwards. Those of you who want to understand life, must understand it like that, that there is no other solution. You can study as many authors as you want, and I, too, have read the works of some scientists and philosophers, but so far not even one of them has given the correct solution to the contemporary crisis which exists in the world. The way this world was born, in the same way it will die. This world is incorrigible, this order in the world is incorrigible, nothing more. They may put whatever system they want in place; they may preach whatever teaching they want; they may place on it whatever religion they like; the contemporary order of things is incorrigible, the contemporary world is incorrigible, nothing more. That is how the issue is. This is a ship which you have boarded, and you shall pray to God to get to shore safely. If you can get to shore safely, then you shall watch out that you never set your foot on it again. If you board a modern steamship I understand it. (The steamship is a figure of speech.)

5, p. 403

In my view, reality is only that thing, upon which I am always the master and which cannot escape from my control. This thing, which can always appear and disappear, is not real. You dream at night that you are rich, but you get up in the morning and you do not have any wealth. You dream that you have an ox, but you get up in the morning and you do not have any ox. In real life this is the same thing. You have hundreds of thousands of leva, but something happens, and you lose them. You are a learned man, but something hits you over the head, and you lose your knowledge. Where is life then? We live in the world of constant change; but then you will say like the present day scientists, that when a man dies, everything is finished with him. There is no need to talk about this. That everything is finished, this is the order of things. It is not bad, that some things are finished. What must be finished? It is good to be finished with disease, because health will come. It is good to be finished with ignorance, because knowledge will come. It is good to be finished with death, because life will come.

5, p. 403

Today, on Earth, there is too large a population than what it should be for people to live happily. As an objection to this they cite the verse from the Bible: "Be fruitful and multiply!" *(Genesis 1: 28)* However, it is not for the foolish and bad people to multiply, but rather for the good people to multiply; we need more reasonable people, we need good people, we need genius people. They should multiply. Why do we need common people in the world for? When the genius, the good and the reasonable people come, they will put the world right, but the common people are little children, who only want to eat and drink. You say, more children are needed. Why are more children required to be born? More children, they say are a blessing. If you are a farmer and you only have one thousand square meters of land, and you have 10 children, 5 daughters and 5 sons, how are you going to care for them? Or if you only have 1,000 leva a month and you have 10 children, how are you going to cope with them? How are you going to go through all these difficult economic situations? How will you dress them, how will you feed them? These children will drain you dry.

5, p. 410

Teachers, priests, statesmen, mothers and fathers, reasonable and good people must come to set the world right. This way the world can be set right, the other way with written laws the world cannot be put right.

5, p. 411

Only on the Divine, that gives you an urge, you must always trust. The other things are good, but the Divine is the seed, the Divine is the power, the Divine is happiness of human life. Upon the Divine rests the health and the happiness of human life, from one end of life to the other end of life.

5, p. 414

All sufferings are external methods, healing methods which adjust our centers, which solve all contradictions and then comes one already different and nice life. The nice and good life consist in living on good terms. You cannot understand one man, until you have about him, one right thought, or said in human language, until you love him. With that, in this love, you must have the desire not to put on him any restrictions.

5, p. 419

In faith one can live only with a reasonable man, but with a foolish man, one cannot live in faith. There is no trust there. The reasonable man is the document himself. With the reasonable people I talk in one way, but with the others, not that they are foolish, I talk in a different way. The first people think to accomplish, in them there is humanity, but in the others there is human selfishness.

5, p. 421

If I explain to you what the just man must be, I will offend myself and you. People today talk about justice, but about the justice of the wolf and the justice of the fox. After skinning the lamb and dividing it, the wolf gave the inner parts to the fox, but for himself he kept the rest of the lamb and then they talked about who has the right over which parts. The wolf has the right and the fox has the right, but what is the right of the lamb, they do not ask.

5, p. 421

You should be in conflict with no man, neither with yourself, nor with your neighbors, your children, your wife or your friends. Why? Because this evening the Lord can summon you. What are you going to tell Him then? Some of you may believe in this, some may not, it makes no difference in what one or another believes.

5, p. 427

For me there is only one society, those people who live in Love, they only comprise the Divine society and this society cannot be ours or yours. Each, who lives in Love is ours. Each one who does not live in Love is yours. You ask, how will the world be set right? The world will be set right when it becomes ours. If it is yours, it won't be set right. You want somebody to be yours. In the words, the world is ours, I mean that I can bring in everything for the benefit of my neighbors. When I refuse to bring in everything, then the world is yours. You say, the world is yours. No, the world is ours. This means, the world of Love is ours. That is how I look at things. By way of continuous manifestations. For me, life does not lie in this, to be good for a day only or for a single moment only. I want in each consecutive moment to keep that condition of good disposition, which I have had earlier. The issue is not to have a good disposition just for a single moment towards the man and to welcome him, but rather whenever I see him, in each moment to be ready to welcome him. Not only this, but I, in my feelings every day, I must feel that I have a certain gain. This gain is not to be in reduction, but in an increase. This is our day.

5, p. 428

There are conditions when crimes cannot be committed, but there are conditions, when a man can always commit crimes. The first crime in the world is to smear a man.

5, p. 429

In the world only one reality exists, from which we cannot take even a single particle for ourselves. So, where will we take it? We live and move in God. Everything, what we see and what we have, is Divine.

5, p. 430

Crime lies in another place. It lies where people do not even suspect it. The crime lies in this, that people are not conductors of pure thoughts. That is the reason for the crimes.

5, p. 437

All crimes are due to the impure thoughts and wishes, which leaves in people certain impurities and excesses.

5, p. 437

I ask, what are the foundations for a man to be executed? Man, who has not created man, does he have the right to execute him? God, Who has created him has the right to dispose with his life, but man does not have any right to dispose of somebody else's life. A potter, who has made a pot, he has the right to break it and make it again. He can break it 20-30 times and make it again. However, the one, who does not know how to make pottery, does he have the right to break them? He does not have the right. If he breaks one pot, he must pay for it.

5, p. 439

In my view, society can be put in order when people's consciousness is uplifted, because one consciousness permeates the other. The smaller consciousnesses form the bigger ones and live in them. God is one consciousness into which all other consciousnesses live. He strives to regulate all these consciousnesses in Himself.

5, p. 440

The knowledge that you have acquired from thousands of years, will determine your next form, that will be given to you. All the animals, which now live on Earth, are all reasonable beings. According to their development, each one will take its corresponding form. The ox cannot not be an ox; the horse cannot not be a horse, the mosquito cannot not be a mosquito; man cannot not be a man. Each will take such a form, to wherever he has arrived within his development. Consequently, the form of each living being must change; it will change in accordance with the degree of the development of their consciousness. In the word consciousness I mean the Divine laws, which function in life.

5, p. 441

Contemporary people say that Love is an empty thing. No one has checked out Love yet, it is still not tried out. The only benefit that people constantly seek everywhere, is Love. They look for it everywhere. They cannot find it, because they want to materialize it, to catch it and to put it in a harness, to do with it whatever they want, that is why you say, that there is no love or that Love is an empty thing. Does the cow that gives her milk, have no love? Does the apple tree, that gives its fruits have no love? For the given moment that is love. That is how God is manifested in all forms of His genesis.

5, p. 441

If in a given moment you do a good deed to somebody, that good deed is common for all. If you do a good deed to some being, who is suffering, that good deed is distributed to all other beings. If one being suffers, that suffering is distributed among all beings. Our sufferings affect all other beings, as a consequence of that, they strive to remove these sufferings, because they too are affected by them. For sure they are not affected like us with the same strength, but they do not want to get any shocks. Take, for example, when a train accident occurs. The accident affects most those who are in the first cars of the train, but the last cars feel only some shaking. So, the advanced beings, too, receive from our sufferings small shakings, but they do not want to get even that much. Now let's go back to the essentials.

Now I do not want to tell you that life is one misfortune or that the sufferings are the greatest evil. Relatively it is like that, but from a Divine point of view, there is something good in the sufferings, which people do not understand. From all the sufferings in which you are enduring now, you will see that one day from them will come out something good. In the scriptures it is said, that everything that happens to those who love the Lord, one day it all will be transformed for their own good. If not in this moment, then that good will come in the next moment.

5, p. 441

They say, that mothers love their children. The contemporary science refutes this to some extent. There are mothers who really love their children a lot, but there are mothers who barely tolerate them. They leave their children to others to bring them up. Some mothers give their children to different institutions, there to be brought up. There are mothers, who are ideal. I do not deny that, but there are mothers, who are not ideal, and from those mothers many troubles have been born into the world. What kind of mother is the one, who cannot teach her son or daughter how to think and to understand the meaning of life? What kind of father is the one, who cannot teach his son or daughter how to think and to understand the meaning of life? Many mothers are like cuckoos; they leave it to others to raise their children. What scientist is this one, who cannot teach and have people learn how to think and to understand the meaning of life? What kind of preacher is this, who, when preaching to people, cannot teach and have them learn how to think and to understand the meaning of life? If the issue is about spending our life as actors, that is a different issue, then I agree with it. However, if the acting does not solve the issues, it is only entertainment, it is only a break.

5, p. 443

Now I can give you one sermon, like the other preachers, I can tell you, live in accordance with Christ's rules! In my view, in order to tell you that you do not live as you should, I must show you how to live, to show you a personal example. I have to definitely give you an example. All Masters, who have come in the world, are distinguished only by this, that they have given people a personal example of how they must live. Christ is distinguished by this, that everything that He had, He gave away. He gave an example. He gave all things that have been tested. He was saying: "This which I have been taught, is what I speak to you." *(John 12: 49)* If the world had gone along Christ's road, at least 95% of all our difficulties, would have disappeared.

5, p. 445

Many have come and have told me, "Tell us that magic law, through which we can pave a way for anywhere." I can tell you this magic key, but I say, here is where the magic lies, love your neighbor.

5, p. 446

So, in the present day conditions, it is peoples' duty to study the language of the human soul. Today people do not talk in the same language. They speak in many languages. People must come to the Divine language, in which all will understand each other. This is the language of Love, which some do not want to learn, but some knew it and now have almost forgotten it. All people must take up the learning of the language of Love. I have made many experiments with dogs. Some dog meets me, looks at me, does not bark at me.

He looks at me, he expects something from me. If I tell myself that I won't give him anything, it will give me a grumpy look, but if I put my hand in my pocket and give him something to eat, he becomes my friend. If this continues a few times, our friendly relations solidify. When you do some favor to a dog, he is ready to be in your disposition. Everyone might have tried this experiment. If you do a favor to a man he will say, "I am ready to do you a favor. The little useful thing that I have, I am ready to share half of it with you." Thus you will form a connection. Christ says: "Love your neighbor like yourself." *(Mark 12: 31)* Divide half of the good things that you have with your neighbor. When you enter with your neighbor into this law, then comes the second law, according to which, "Where there are two or three gathered in my name, there I am too." *(Matthew 18: 20)* Where Love is among two or three, God is there. Where God is, all things move forward. This is the First law, which all people must learn. When they learn these situations, we will arrange the other issues, because Love is required everywhere: in societies, in nations, in political parties and in families. Love must enter as a measurement everywhere, because it reconciles things. Love will soften the hearts of the rulers so they feel the situation of the workers. Love will also soften the hearts of the workers so they feel the situation of their rulers. If Love enters into people's consciousness as a factor, they will enter in the right way of that natural development, which people and all nations as well seek. There is no other way. This path has been tested. The idea about God can be passed on to others inasmuch as I apply it to myself. It is not about what I believe, but is in this, which comes from me. People believe so much in a spring, as much water comes out from it. From the water that comes out of it, its price is determined. It is all according to the quality of the water. If this springs stops giving water, it loses its price. If the water of the spring increases, it gains higher price. Consequently, as much as we become conductors of God's Love to come out from us, our value increases.

"He who studies the Word of God." studying the Word of God, this is what we have to work upon in the future. This is with which we can build our lives.

5, p. 448

In Love things are real, but outside of Love they are unreal. Love is the great, the reality in the world.

5, p. 456

When a soul is awakened, it has started to seek Love.

5, p. 456

I do not connect love with marriage. Marriage is a trade deal. Love is a Divine process, which is common for all of nature. It is a continuous process in the whole cosmic genesis, in all beings from the smallest to the biggest. Marriage among the angels does not exist. If an angel in heaven decides to get married, they will be kick it out from there. If two angels tell each other one rude word, as people in marriage do, nothing will be left for them. There is not even remembrance of rude words there. Angels do not have such experiences as people do. Angels are like people they are without wings, they are good people, extremely reasonable, who understand the deep meaning of nature's laws. They have tremendous power, they can project their 25 million wings, like an airplane. Angels can fly with a speed greater than that of light. In a short time an angel can go through the space, to go from one location to another. Not that all angels are extremely reasonable and they are on different levels of development among themselves, but in comparison with people they stand much higher. Similarly, between people there are different levels of development.

5, p. 457

He who has knowledge, will be a strong man. If you are a weak man, you do not have any knowledge. If you are scared of the sufferings, you are a weak man. Suffering is the negative side of life. To protect yourself from the most unfavorable conditions that could have happened in your life, of which you can come across, only Love can give you that protection. That, which can support your life, is Love, which must be looked at from all sides.

5, p. 458

That which, in a given situation, can restore your state of health, to make you an independent man and to free you from the restrictions, that is the reality. Everything else I call conditions in life. Money, for example is one condition, strength is one condition, knowledge is a condition, richness is a condition. Those things I do not deny, but I say, what is real in the world is that which gives strength and power to man, that is Love, the Divine in man, which must be proclaimed.

5, p. 459

When Love enters you, you feel like the whole universe is in you. You already are receiving and listening to the Love of all beings. Their Love and your Love are one and the same. Then you hear the voice of all angels, all saints and all beings in the world and they all say, what a great meaning there is in life.

5, p. 459

Somebody says, I do not need riches. The issue is not there. You can be the richest man in the world, but the evil is not in the riches. The evil lies in the lack of understanding of life, because each wealth is one opportunity for you. The wealth has meaning, to become through it a conductor of the great, to help your neighbors and then the knowledge which we have and the strength which we have and the goodness which we have, everything that we have, for everything we are conductors, sent from the invisible world to help those, who are in need. This does not mean the whole world, but in a given situation at least to a small circle of people. What is nicer than this, if you can show your Love. However, you wait for others to love you. This is good, it is not bad for people to love you. However, there are two things in life which I consider the best. There is nothing better in life than to be loved and there is nothing better than to love. These are the nicest, the best things, to be loved and to love. To appreciate it when you are loved and to be appreciated, when you love. Meaning, you shall appreciate the Love of the one who loves you and the one who you love, to appreciate your Love.

5, p. 460

The brains of scientists are bigger, heavier than the brains of the ignorant people. Regarding the body, it must be known that it is not the man, it just represents the man's cloth.

5, p. 463

I consider in me the moral that thing, that gives benefit simultaneously to me and to my neighbors. If something is truthful towards me, it must be truthful to others as well.

5, p. 466

If you think that the Lord does everything, it will be discovered that He is in contradiction with Himself. The Lord cannot be in contradiction with Himself. As a man and I cannot be in contradiction with myself. If I am in contradiction with myself, the reason is somewhere outside. It is impossible for a man to be in conflict with himself. Man can get in conflict with himself only when one external cause, one little circumstance, interferes with him.

5, p. 466

If religion does not make us conductors of God's Love and does not make us to serve people, to show them God's Love, then that religion is not worth even a nickel. If religion cannot create great, good, powerful people, who can bring order and ordinance everywhere, what type of religion is that?

If you however say that people must leave the old ways, they do not like that. I put myself in the shoes of the people who live with Love for the old, but there are certain scientific discoveries, new ones, which must be accepted. In man there is one higher sense, which is located on top, in the center, of the head, that senses, the Indians call one thousand leaves. That sense is a center of the higher consciousness in man, a center of his Love of God.

5, p. 473

In what lies man's dignity? One of the qualities of human dignity lies in the right thought. Another quality of his dignity is honesty, and the third quality is his goodness. These are the three qualities necessary for human dignity: goodness (ability to be good in his dealings with others), honesty and the right thought. This is what a man's dignity is distinguished by. There are other qualities, but these three are most prominent. Consequently, every man who destroys your good, he cannot be a good man for you; every man, who destroys your honesty, he cannot be good for you and every man who destroys your right thought, he is not a good man for you. This is a rule, through which you can know which man is right, who is a good man and who is not a good man.

5, p. 478

Everything that man has done wrong can be corrected. Man's strength lies in this, to correct anything that he has done wrong sometime in the past. This is possible.

5, p. 487

When Christ says: "If you do not eat my flesh," *(John 6: 53)* through this eating namely is known His Love. This means, from the Word, that I am giving you, you will accept the Word and you will know my Love. If during two thousand years we had accepted Christ's teachings in its simplicity, it would have had tremendous results in the whole of your life. Now we want to apply Christ's teachings, to adjust it in accordance with the surrounding environment, so while supporting it, we are not considered abnormal by the people. In what lies the norm in the world? The only norm with which things are measured in the world, is Love. The only norm, with which knowledge is measured, is Love. The only norm with which justice is measured, is Love. Everywhere in the foundation of all aspirations in the whole of nature is Love. You go to fight for your fatherland, because you love it. In a given case the sacrifice which you want to make is due to the Love you have. Whether you correctly understand Love or not, is another issue. In the given case for Love is wanted motivational reasons. You support religion, this is Love; you support science, this is Love.

5, p. 488

Christ says: "If your justice, if your love does not surpass this of the ordinary people, you will not enter the Kingdom of God, you do not have life in yourselves." *(Matthew 5: 47)* If you are not ready to do anything for the Divine Love, you have no life in yourself. In order to do anything, you must free yourself from one inner fear, from one inner feeling. For example, you have good wishes, but the fear in you stops these wishes. You decide to do something, but you immediately ask yourself, but what will happen to me? The worst that can happen to you is this, that you will lose your temporary life. Or you will suffer or get sick and you will die. For example, you support certain religious beliefs, but you do not want to die. Many martyrs have denied Christ, when the sufferings and the torment come, they then say, we do not believe in Christ. What did they gain when they denied Christ? Did they keep their lives? Definitely not. They died anyway. When it comes to speaking the truth, no one is forcing you to say whom you love and whom you do not. Man must be fair to himself, he must feel that Love. Regardless of what people say, he must know that he loves God, nothing more. All what he is ready to do for himself, he must be ready to do it for that Love, too. All people must have this moral. This moral is not for one person, it is for all people. This is the Divine Beginning, the moral in us, if we think like that (But what will happen to me?). God will never manifest Himself in us, He will not act in us. Many seek God outside. No, God manifests himself and in the believers and in the unbelievers. He manifests Himself in all people. Somebody does not believe in God, but God whispers in his heart to go help someone who is suffering, and he goes and helps him. Sometimes, God goes and whispers in the heart of some believer to go help someone who is suffering, but he says, I do not have time now, I am going to pray. Often the unbelievers listen to God more often and help the suffering people, than the believers, who are busy with themselves. Which is more important, to do the Will of God or to go to God and tell Him, that you love Him a lot? Which is more important, to tell the Lord, that you love Him a lot and that you believe in Him or to go and fulfill His Will? To serve God is more important, from your faith in Him and your love of Him. The three together, doing His Will, having faith in Him and love for Him, that is the reality of Love.

5, p. 489

Education is necessary so man can climb up to a higher level. Do not think that you do not need to study. Studying is necessary for man. The whole world is one great school, not only the Earth, but the whole solar system and all other systems as well, represent prominent faculties. There are a number of cultures, each one more wonderful than the other.

(The term *"faculty"* in Bulgaria is used to describe studies/departments of education in higher educational institution like universities. Examples of faculties: Faculty or history, faculty of theology, faculty of biology, faculty of mathematics and informatics and etc.)

5, p. 492

Christ says: "If you do not eat my flesh and do not drink my blood, you do not have life in yourselves." This means, if you do not accept that Love, if you do not accept that sacrifice, which I make, you do not have life in yourselves.

5, p. 494

If you get discouraged, sing; thus you will gradually come out of your discouragement, from your faithlessness. Faithlessness always comes from the loss of something. Faith always comes from a gain. Lovelessness comes from a loss. Love comes from a gain. Consequently, if you lose your

Love, this shows that you have incurred some loss. If Love is coming, this shows, that some gain is coming. If the loss represents climbing down, the gain represents climbing up. That is how I reason. Consequently, when you lose something you are descending. When you gain something you are ascending.

5, p. 495

Do not think that you are old. You shall know, that your head is old, but your body is young. Then have faith, love and do the Will of God! These are the first steps of the new culture, of the new humanity, of the new understanding, of the new closeness among the nations. Each nation must believe in other nations. Each nation must love other nations, and each nation must serve other nations. If the small nations think and believe in the big ones, if people of all nations love each other and serve each other, this will be good for all sides and for their neighbors as well

5, p. 495

If you want to know whether the Lord thinks about you, do the following experiment. Go to a sick person and say, Lord, if it is written like that, may this sick person be healed. You will see that after two or three days this sick person will be healthy. When this thing happens, that means you have received an answer to your prayer. What else do you have doubt with? You are neither a saint, nor a righteous man, but you received an answer to your prayer. Then the doubt will come. That man was healthy earlier or maybe his health would have been restored anyway. Make the same experiment one more time. If you doubt, you will be put sick in a bed and your life will be hanging by a thread.

5, p. 504

How are mistakes set right? When you study! God created the world for certain souls to study and to progress. Consequently, birth, rebirth, death, all these are opportunities in the world for the progress and the development of those souls. We have not come for happiness on Earth. Happiness is outside of life. Before coming on Earth, all people were happy. The reality is this, that those souls had to come down from heaven and to bring something for the other people. Do you think that Christ was not happy? He was happy and the richest of all people, but He left His happiness and came down on Earth among the sinners and suffering people to show them the way, upon which they must develop.

Now I want you to look only at the real things, in these be interested, but in those, which do not exist, do not spend your time. I am talking to you about things that I know, but whether you believe in them or not, it is another issue. There are things, which I have tried 999 times and in which I live, but there are things, which do not exist for me. For example, Good is something real for me. Justice is something real for me, the good people are something good for me. I have made a number of observations and have come to the conclusion, that in certain conditions the worst people can show very good traits. There are cases, in which the best people can show the worst traits.

5, p. 507

God's Love is known by this, that it is ready for all sacrifices. When you love man in a human way, you will see in him the bad things, but if you love him in a Divine way, you will never see in him anything bad; you will see only the good in man. All misunderstandings, everything in life is due to this, that people walk upon the path of human Love, but life in this way cannot be corrected. Until now people have walked along the way of the human, the personal Love, which has created many things in the world, but it cannot bring happiness to people. Man must come to the so called cosmic Love or the Love of the soul. The Love of the soul must be shown in order for the world to be set right.

5, p. 509

In my view, happiness is achievable only with Love. Without Love, no happiness in the world can exist. When sometimes we are happy, it is due to our temporary look through the rays of Love. When those rays disappear, the same unhappiness and darkness sets in us again.

Now I see that my thoughts are a little bit in the abstract for you. They are in the abstract, for the only reason that Love is absent in you, for you to understand them.

5, p. 511

You have not studied yet the life of the other world so that you know what a man needs after he dies. Many think, that when one dies, he starts thinking only about heaven. The dead do not like it at all for people to talk bad about them, they do not like bad thoughts to be thrown about, regarding them. Why do they not like it? Even without it, they are already judging themselves. They already see their mistakes and are suffering, therefore you do not need to add anything to their sufferings. If they have done something good to you, keep that good always in your mind. If you want to make one good connection with a man or whoever it could be, a saint or even with somebody who has departed, keep in your mind at least one good trait of theirs. Thus you will find God. Somebody wants to find God, but he comes with all of his critical thoughts. Thus you cannot find God. Thus God is not sought

5, p. 511

Man is not allowed to mock the name of God or the name of Christ. Be aware of one thing, man must be extremely careful when he is presented in a case to explain the truth. Regarding the truth, regarding the saints, regarding the great people, you must be extremely careful, otherwise your results will be bad. Do not just say, that God is Love, but you must also tell yourself, God is just and I must be just like Him. God is generous and I must be generous. God is good and I must be good. God wants from us, as His children, to be like Him. It is said in the Scripture: "Let your deeds be illuminated before God's face." *(Matthew 5: 16)*

5, p. 512

When it comes to the name of God, you must show yourself with all of your purity and justice. You say, "Love is a dangerous thing, it is a fire, it burns people's hearts." There is no burning in Love. Love brings health, strength, knowledge, wealth (spiritual meaning too) and other good traits. When it comes to Love you say, beware of it, because it twists people's minds. In my view, wherever Love enters, it straightens out people's minds, and everything starts going "on honey and butter" (BG expression, meaning very smooth). That's how it is with the Divine Love. When your things are not going on honey and butter, you are not with any Love. We are expecting that Love is now coming into the world. This Love is in the Word of God, in His light. This Love must come now into the world. You must see that the One, Who loves you, Who has passed from death into life, the only One, Who shows His Love: that is Christ.

5, p. 512

I will give you one rule. Never give a feast to people who have a full stomach, if you want your head to be at peace. By no means give a feast to the people who have a full stomach. If you want to give a feast to somebody, find hungry people and provide a feast to them. You will have God's blessing. When you provide a feast to the full man, he will do you some mischief. You, by no means, can feed the man who is full. He will be extremely demanding, saying that this or that is not good. If you want to feed somebody, wait for some traveler in the mountains. If you give him a piece of bread, this will have greater meaning for you, than if you give a feast to the full man.

Now I am looking at the things in their inner meaning.

5, p. 514

Sometimes man is full and wants to eat again. With this he is committing a crime. But wait, let me eat a little so nothing bad happens to me. No, eat only when you are hungry. When Christ was in the desert, the devil came and tempted Him and told Him, make these stones into bread! Christ replied to him: "All people, who have eaten from the bread of stones have died. And this bread, which people now eat, is again from the stones. The soil which you now cultivate, is all from stones made. And even if I make bread, people will still die from it. However, if they feed themselves with the Word of God, they will not die. People must learn to feed themselves with every Word, that comes out of the mouth of God." Sometimes, it seems strange to people, that they can feed themselves with the Word of God. For all those who do not understand these things, for them there are strange things out there. He, whose heart has never felt what Love is, it is strange for him to be talked to about Love.

5, p. 515

In order for a man to critique others, he must have 12 senses in himself, to see things clearly. Contemporary people, barely have 5 senses, they do not even have 7 senses developed. Consequently, they have not come even half way in their development.

5, p. 518

For the time being, man is the last creation on Earth. Consequently, because the water, the ground, the air and the light, were created before him, they are created for him. If you do not understand why this world was created, then what are you going to understand? I do not say, that you do not understand anything. You understand many things, but I ask you: do you understand God's language? Do you talk His language? In the Divine language there is not even one negative word. In the Divine language the words: "I cannot" do not exist. In the Divine language the words faithlessness and lovelessness do not exist. In the Divine language only positive words exist. There, each word has only one meaning and when you say that word, it happens. You go to pray in your language, and are wondering why there is no answer to your prayers. When you pray to God, He does not understand you. Now even the most advanced beings, in order to go to the Lord, in order for their prayers to be accepted, they must pray for 20 years. Even the greatest saints are babblers before the Lord. This is not humiliation. They, for years, babble before the Lord, like children, till they learn how to pray. With that they pass for great saints before the people.

5, p. 518

A saint is he who looks with a good eye on everything. Whatever he sees, he knows that it is God's deed, but God's deeds for him are right. That one, whose cheeks are hollow and his eyes are hollow is not a saint. He is a sick man, not a saint. The face of the saint is not yellowish, but instead gives out light, especially at night. The saint will always find you when you are in a difficult situation and will give you light on your path. He will show you the way and again will go on with doing his things. The saints are interpreters of God's Law. They teach people how to talk. They are masters of humanity, they teach the Divine language. When you meet a saint, first you shall let him to teach you the alphabet of the Divine language, and then he will start teaching you the words, the most simple ones, which you can understand. When you pronounce one word, you will see that things will happen. When you say the word "apple" in the Divine language, at once the apple tree will be before you, and its fruits will ripen right before your eyes. When you say the word, "house," at once, before you will show a palace, whatever one you want. When you say, "piano," you will have the best piano. You will sit down and you will play it. When you say the word "virtuoso," you will become one, whatever one you want. Whatever you say, that's what it will be. You ask, how's that possible? For some of you this could happen only after 8 thousand years. For some of you this can happen after one thousand years, for a third after 500 years, for a fourth, after one hundred years, for a fifth after one year, but for some, maybe after 1-2 months.

5, p. 519

If you are in camaraderie with a bad man, you will not do well, nothing will be left from you. To be in camaraderie with a bad man, you definitely must be stronger than him. I have seen many cases where in such a camaraderie nothing has been achieved. Man cannot easily overcome the forces that come out from the bad man. If the issue is to overcome that which is in you by coping with it alone, there is no need to seek the bad man outside, he is inside you. Everyone has noticed how difficult it is for a man to be pacified, when the hatred in the man rises up. When hatred, pride, suspicion, ill will, bitterness, faithlessness, rise up, it is very hard for a man to overcome all these things. Even the most righteous man sometimes is exposed to temptation. These are tests, through which man's character is tested. The sin does not lie in this, that hatred has passed through the human heart. The sin lies in this, when you accept hatred in the three worlds: the physical, the spiritual and in the mental world, then you get tied up (you lose your freedom).

5, p. 522

Oftentimes you stop to think over the issue which people are good and which are bad. Put aside the bad people, God will deal with them, there is no need for you to cope with them. Except God, no one else is in the condition to cope with bad people. Remember this thing. Christ has said, *"do not resist evil." (Matthew 5: 39)* Everyone who has tried to fight with evil, he has always paid with his life. God understands the law, only He has the power to fight and cope with evil.

5, p. 522

Love lies in this, to find out in man one good trait, and when you find that trait, to be glad about it. In the one, whom you do not love, you see in him only his bad traits. If you see his good traits, you will uplift him. We need people who can find not the bad, but the good traits in man, and when they find the good traits, to hold them in front of themselves. Christ came in the world to show the good in man.

5, p. 527

Every change in the physical world is connected with some change in the spiritual world, and every change in the spiritual world is connected with some change in the mental world. Or said in another way, the change in the thoughts and the feelings tells us about the change in the actions as well. The actions are connected with the thoughts and with feelings. Consequently, the actions represent an end, one finished result.

5, p. 531

In my view, man first studies, and when he has learned he begins to love. Since only the smart man can love, but the fool never. Consequently, Love, according to my understanding, is not a science for the foolish people, it is a science only for the smartest people.

5, p. 533

To be a religious man you must learn how to think, you must purify your feelings, so they become as pure as a crystal, and you must act absolutely justly. In you, there must not exist even a single hair of injustice. This is what it means to be a religious man.

5, p. 540

Christianity does not allow any inheritance wills to be made. Whatever the father gives to his son, he should give it while he is living; he should not leave any inheritance wills so they have a quarrel after his death. Whatever is left, he is to keep it for himself or give it to others the way he sees it. So now what happens is he will leave to his son an inheritance so they make him a memorial service, to bury him nicely, but afterwards brothers and sisters will quarrel among themselves. That is what they call Christianity. Those are pagan traditions. That has its own origins. I say all these sins are built from one wrongful teaching, from a wrongful understanding.

5, p. 543

Now, when I talk to you, someone says, we believe in what the Master says. No, I do not want that, but I say, until you do not come to believe in the Divine teaching, until you do not check out things, you cannot know anything. There are certain principles, which must be applied and tried. It is a sin if they are not applied. Christ says: "If you love me, you will keep my commandments." *(John 14: 15)* The contemporary believers must know that. It all depends on our faith, on our Love, on our thoughts. We have the strength within ourselves to set our lives right. There is no difficulty in the world, which we cannot set right. If the weather outside is cold, it is just enough for the believers to pray for the weather to warm up and it will. If there is a storm and they pray, the storm will stop; if there is poverty and they pray, the poverty will go away. If there are diseases and they pray, the diseases will stop; if there are Earthquakes, they will stop; if there are clouds, they will be scattered. In small numbers many Christians have tried this thing, but they find this thing very difficult, because work is needed. When it comes to praying, people think that one man can do it all. Everyone can do the things exactly as needed if he works in accordance with the great Divine law. You do a good thing in the world, and all those souls who have felt your good one day will repay you; they will be close people to you. There are no exceptions in this. Whatever good you do in the world, this good will be a benefit for all people. Those people who are affected by your good, one day will repay you. Do not get discouraged, have faith in your beliefs, wish good to people regardless of whether you know them or not. Do good to people through your faith despite not knowing them. When you do good, call upon Love. When you act like that, people's good will come to you. Or the good that they send you will pass through you to other people and then again will return back to you.

5, p. 545

People think that God does not get angry. God gets angry and people will experience his anger. When God gets angry, the world will be set on fire, but then will be set right. If God does not get angry, the world will not be set right.

5, p. 553

Until then, when your views change, you are not in the reality of life. Until then, when your views change, you will not have any achievements. The law is true and in the physical, the spiritual and in the Divine world. In order to have any achievements, you must be in the reality of life. When you come to the real, to the essential in yourself, you can expect an achievement. Reality lies in the unity of thought. Until then, until you are divided in two in your heart and in your mind, until then, your wishes, your aspirations, your prayers cannot be achieved. Such are at least the experiences of all those who live in the past. But when a man's consciousness unites, when his heart and mind unite, and he does not have any contradictions in his mind and his heart, he can expect achievements. Outside of this, he cannot expect any achievements. For example, you want to do something good, but something in your soul says, that you will not succeed. When there are no contradictions in your mind, and you are sitting firm like a rock, as if it is on the Himalayas, you must know that what the Spirit has told you from within, it will be.

5, p. 553

Never stop at the contradictions in life. What are they, and why have they come? You can stop at the contradictions, but only, when you have free time. When you have no free time, do not stop at the contradictions to solve them. For example, it can be hard to solve why some people are good, but others are bad. It is hard to determine what are the causes, that some people are good, but others bad. Sometimes, you feel in yourself one indisposition, but you cannot give to yourself an account of that indisposition. That you are in indisposition, this you see, but you cannot give yourself an account of what that indisposition is due to. I say, if I put you in a room facing south with abundance of light, with enough food and enough entertainment, it will be pleasant to us. If you are put in a room facing north, without windows, which is humid and without light, your disposition will change. In the same way you can make from your thoughts a chalet, in which you will get sick. From those negative thoughts you will create around yourself one unhealthy aura or one completely unhygienic dwelling.

5, p. 554

It is not the issue, in the present day life, to judge ourselves for our actions, it is not the issue to say to what level a person has progressed. There is progress only in Love. There is progress only in the Truth. There is progress only in the knowledge. All other things in which there is no truth, no knowledge, no Love; in them there is no progress. In another way man cannot progress. In progress we understand a gain, no matter how small or how microscopic it is. In progress where there is no gain, we are not interested in this progress.

5, p. 556

The natural situation when you talk to a man, is for him to look you straight in the eye, not to stare, but freely and calmly look at you. A man who looks you straight in the eye is a free man and it is a pleasure to look at such a man. Therefore, it is good for a man every day to do one exercise to keep his head upright. You are sitting, thinking about something and looking downwards, do not keep your eyes downwards, but rather, turn them up.

5, p. 556

Whether in the evening or daytime you are praying, lift your eyes up. He, who wants to be a Christian, he who wants to be a nobleman, he who wants to pray, he must lift his eyes up.

5, p. 557

All people want to be loved. How will you be loved? In order to be loved, you must possess some virtues, some qualities, either in the physical world or in the spiritual world or in the Divine world or in the mental world. Without these qualities you cannot be loved. You can be loved for your body, your heart and your mind; for the time being, this is how it is in this life. If you however have these three things simultaneously and they love for them, their Love for you will be natural.

5, p. 559

Love is the greatest bliss, the greatest good, if only a man can accept it.

5, p. 560

All things that are being lost are not from Divine character. They are of human nature; and therefore you should not feel sorry for them. They are in their place, but because man has already set his foot in the Divine, he must not stop at them. If we do not pass through the human way, we cannot enter into the Divine.

5, p. 560

Do not worry, because God has created the world as one great school and regardless of whatever contradictions are given to you, do not worry. The worries will come, but do not stop before them. I have often been told, it is easy to say, "Do not worry." However, if you worry, what will you gain? You have broken your leg, you will fix it. You will be suffering for some time, the leg will get healed, it will be fine, there is no danger. Somebody lost ten thousand or a hundred thousand leva, he will suffer a bit and he will gain it again. However, it is not lost anywhere, the money will come again. When the righteous loses a thousand leva, he will gain ten thousand; when the sinner gains a thousand leva, he will lose ten thousand leva. According to my statistics, it is like that. When the righteous one goes through great suffering, for him it is one good thing. In the Scripture it is said: "Everything will transform to good for those who love God." *(Romans 8: 28)* Sometimes, you hesitate and you say, whether my credo is right. If the credo is not right, find the right credo. Am I near Paradise? You have to find out. Where will you learn that? When I go to school, I must study, to finish well. This is what you have to say to your teacher, I know, that when I study, the professor will reward me, and I will pass into the higher grade. However, if I do not study and if I stay in the same class for two-three years, just by staying, one cannot pass to a higher grade. Some say, we have been listening for ten years, what kind of thing is this, that we have not finished it yet? We are on the right path aren't we? Then who is in the wrong? Am I in the wrong? Tell us at least one way how to do it. We have been listening for so long. By listening, you cannot build a creed within yourself and by imposing, and a creed cannot be acquired either. You can believe in what I believe, because you are walking along the same path, but the difference between you and me is this, that I believed early and started in this way; from the very first word I believed, but you sit and ask whether I was lied to.

5, p. 561

You have contradictions in the individual, family and social life, but in all these contradictions only God is in the power to pull you out 100%; all other hopes are palliative. In the Scripture it is said: "I was young, grew old and did not see justice." *(Psalm 37: 25)* Whoever walks in the ways of God, he cannot be in deprivation. To you I say, go along this path and do not be discouraged.

5, p. 562

I recommend you to fall in love with God, He has things to give you. He will give you the whole moon in a dowry. Everyone, who falls in love with God, will have so much in abundance that he will never be in deprivation.

5, p. 563

There are three important rules, which you must keep in your mind, in order to free yourself from all of your delusions. **The first rule is: Love is a way in life.** If you want to free yourself from all delusions, you have to walk upon the way of Love. If you are not in the way of Love, the greatest mishaps will come upon you. **The second rule is: The Light of Wisdom is a way of knowledge.** Consequently, if you do not have this way or this light, you cannot acquire knowledge. If you do not have this light of Wisdom, you will not know how to put your life in order, neither will you be able to put in order your things and you will find yourself in eternal contradiction with yourself. **The third rule is: The Truth is a way to freedom.** Consequently, if you are not in this way of truth, you cannot be free. These are maxims, formulas. Why is it like that? It is done, there is no need to ask why. But this thing must be tested. Everyone must try these maxims. We cannot talk about things, which have not been tested by us. Only tested things can be talked about.

5, p. 564

Many of you are talented, you can sing, but you do not know how to sing. Firstly, you cannot sing for the reason, that you are shy and say that people will be laughing at you. I will give you one rule how to sing. Firstly, you will go to sing before the hens. Then you will find a flock of ducks and you will sing to them. Then you will sing to a herd of sheep, to a herd of cattle and in this way you will overcome your fear. Thus you will come to sing before the people. The hens, the ducks, the sheep, this is the audience which will be listening to you. When you overcome your fear, then you will come out and sing before the people. If before your singing, the hens were pecking, but when you begin to sing, they stop pecking and raise their heads up, this shows that they have appreciated your singing.

5, p. 569

When a man does things in accordance with God, he has in his disposition all the good people in the world. When man serves God, wherever he may go, he will have all the doors opened for him.

5, p. 571

The good people, who live in accordance with God, are distinguished with great reason, they are the most reasonable people in the world. Those who live humanly are distinguished by this, that they are the most foolish people in the world. That is the way by which I recognize one kind from the other.

5, p. 571

It is not the issue for the Lord to deal with you, but you have to deal with the Lord. We incorrectly assign the issue. You have to deal with the Lord, to study His language. You shall try once, twice, three times until you understand His language. Then you shall pay attention to the Lord. You shall turn to the Lord to give you whatever you want.

5, p. 574

Now you all want to have one quiet and calm life. Nature does not love a calm life.

5, p. 576

Each one of you must have an excellent concept about life and to stop worrying. Stop worrying about unnecessary things. If God reigns on Earth and if you say that He is your father, what do you have to worry about? Let's assume, you are sick. What bad is there in getting ill or in the illness? This is up to the man's understanding. Or, let's assume, that you are poor. What is the bad in poverty? Or let's assume you become rich. What good is there in the richness? In the poverty there is no evil and in richness there is no good. These are only conditions. Poverty is one condition and richness is another condition. Illness is one condition, good health is another condition. These are conditions, tasks for solving. A man, who understands these conditions, must be above poverty and richness, above erudition and ignorance, above good and evil. Good and evil bring conditions with which man can develop himself. Why does evil exist, this issue cannot be solved. You shall put this issue aside and not deal with it. You cannot deal with Love and with hatred, they are conditions. You must use these conditions. If you do not use them, you cannot solve the issue of why were they created. No matter how much you think, you cannot solve the issue regarding the contradictions. For the learned people, the contradictions have already been resolved. For those, who know and understand things, there are no contradictions. The contradiction only *seems* to be a contradiction.

5, p. 576

If a man does not walk along the path of Love, he cannot have life. If a man does not walk along the way of Wisdom, he cannot have light and knowledge. If a man does not walk along the path of Truth, he cannot have freedom. Truth, this is the way to freedom. In Truth man can be strong. In order for a man to acquire his freedom, he must be strong. The weak cannot be free. The strong can be free. Strong is he, who has life, who has knowledge and he who has the Truth on his side. This man is a free man. This is said theoretically. If we enter the contemporary social life, all sociologists, all who deal with the improvement of contemporary society, the teachers dealing with the inculcation of higher personal qualities of youth and religious people, they all have similar understandings. Religion is needed, but it does not solve all the issues. Education does not solve all the issues. The social sciences solve something, but not everything. The thing which solves everything in life, is Love. Love cannot solve the issues without the way of knowledge. There can be no knowledge without the way of Truth. So, life, knowledge and freedom are results of the primary cause. Life is a result of

Love, knowledge is a result, freedom is one result as well. If behind the result you do not have Love, if behind the knowledge you do not have the Wisdom, if behind the freedom you do not have Truth, you will lose freedom.

5, p. 578

If you are a man who only sees people's mistakes, you are ignorant man. Stop seeing people's mistakes, because they are from a different nature. That somebody has made a mistake; this is a different issue. This mistake is not his. You have a son born, who by inheritance is a drunkard. He is not at fault, his grandfather was drinking, his great-grandfather used to drink and now all say that he is a drunkard. Firstly, he is not a drunkard. His grandfather was drinking first. This man who has knowledge, must go back four generations. It is very difficult for a drunkard to be corrected, who is such by the law of inheritance. It can be corrected, but it is difficult. That habit is very deeply settled in his consciousness.

5, p. 579

Now, I am giving you three rules: Love is to be a way for your life; Wisdom is to be a way for your knowledge and light; Truth is to be a way for your freedom. This is the new science which you must apply as a foundation and with which you will acquire all that you wish for.

5, p. 581

Now I want to lead you to the thought that you have to leave aside the ordinary things in life. The ordinary things create all the mishaps in life. Consequently, the ordinary things are those that create all the mishaps in life. The extraordinary things are those, which create all the happiness in life. Since most people are unhappy, they have entered the ordinary life. You suffer, because you have entered into an ordinary life. Enter into the extraordinary life, if you want to free yourself from sufferings. The ordinary life is distinguished by one's inner immobility. Immobility is one of the conditions, which gives birth to all mishaps. This, that gives an impulse for movement, that is happiness. Always, when happiness comes, you start jumping, you become joyful. When the mishap comes, you bend your head down, you do not move from your place. When good health comes, you get off the bed and start walking. When you are ill, you lie down on the bed and start thinking. Illness is one ordinary condition, but good health is one extraordinary condition. There are a number of philosophers who want to prove what the reasons are for these things. There aren't any. It is all due to misunderstanding. When you do not understand one good man, you will create for yourself a mishap, but when you understand him, you will create your happiness.

5, p. 582

In my view Love is not something like water, nor like sugar, nor like bread for me to take. For me, Love is not something material. Love is the essence of life.

5, p. 586

Somebody doubts in God and says, "Prove to me whether the Lord exists." I tell him, "You prove to me that He does not exist. I have more evidence that God exists than you to the contrary." This world that is surrounding us, is half the proof, that there is something outside us, that exists. What is this thing called coincidence? Coincidence in the world is one big misunderstanding. Only those who accept the coincidences in life, are the ones who do not understand the laws of nature. Only the ordinary people believe in coincidences. Now if I ask you, why did you come on Earth, you won't know what to say. You didn't come on Earth, by your own will. Do you remember when you came? Do you remember that moment, when you came out from heaven? Do you remember the port, at which you came down? Do you remember when your consciousness woke up? You do not even remember the time of 9 months, which you spent in the womb of your mother. You do not remember your birth.

5, p. 590

If we believe in the idea that the Lord has created people, we do not have the right to talk bad things about them.

5, p. 591

The freedom, which God has given us, which the contemporary philosophers do not see, is the cause for all of our mistakes and crimes. It shows, that God has given us this freedom, so we can freely develop ourselves.

5, p. 592

I keep for myself one law, to be always right with myself. To have correct relations with all people. I know one thing positively, that there is no bigger poison than a lie in the world. The scariest thing, of which each man can be afraid of, is the smallest lie. Never try to lie to yourself. When you come to the lie, say to yourself, "This is a lie." In my knowledge, an honest and noble man is he, who does not allow the lie. He may commit a variety of transgressions, but all of them can be forgiven. The only sin which Nature does not forgive is the lie. The first people were kicked out of Paradise, not because of their transgression, but because of their lie. Adam lied to the Lord. He said, "Lord, that woman that you gave me, made me transgress." This was the first lie in the world. When Eve was caught, she said, "The Serpent made me transgress." This is the second lie. From here I say, there are two kinds of lies in the world, female and male lies. ..... Adam was supposed to tell the Lord, Lord, forgive me that I sinned with my partner. I didn't put her to work, but let her deal with external things. I did not bring her before you. That is the truth. However, he wanted to play politics, to have his beloved have a good disposition for him, so she does not form a bad opinion about him. He had a weakness for his beloved, and that weakness took him to the bottom of hell. He wanted to please his woman. This is the first pleasing. She wanted to please her man too. Do not please each other. To please a man, that means to tell him the truth. Nothing more. If I tell you a lie, this is disrespect. When one man tells me lies, he neither respect himself nor me. If I tell you lies, I neither myself respect, nor you. In the new culture man must speak the truth. He who does not know how to speak the truth, I do not know what else he can tell you. If I do not tell you the truth, I do not know what I can say for myself. This means that I neither respect myself nor you. In the new culture man must speak only the truth. If he cannot speak the truth, I do not know what else he can do.

5, p. 595

This is how one must reason. Only when you do good, you will love it.

5, p. 597

Love the good, by doing it.

5, p. 597

The Good you can only love when you are doing it. Consequently, doing good in the world, I call Love.

5, p. 597

If you love God, you must say to yourself, everything, that I am going through, is for the Good. You cannot tell this to anybody, except to yourself. Do not tell it to others, but accept it inside yourself, that it is for the Good. You can seek what is written in the sacred books, what the experiences of the other people are, but do not tell others what you are thinking. Even in the worst conditions, assume that all that is for the Good. When you assume that, you right away will be connected with the first principle, in connection with the Divine. Say to yourself, this which I cannot solve, God will solve. If you say so, you will see, that in less than 24 hours the solution of the issue will come, because it is not you, who solves the issues in the world. This Being, whom I am telling you about and which I know, is not like the ordinary man, who you know, it is not like when you know one man. This Being, towards which all aspire, which arranges everything in life, towards it have benevolence, even the most advanced beings that have knowledge. All aspire towards its benevolence. Why? Whereas it is a spring, which contains, unbounded knowledge, unbounded goods, unbounded happiness in life. Now I am not talking to you about one Lord, in Whom you should just believe. I am not talking to you about one Lord, in Whom people, once upon a time, have believed. My Lord, about Whom I am talking to you today, says, that everything, that you want and expect from Him, He will do. Today you have clouds in your life, but if you believe in this Lord, you will have fewer clouds in your life, your sky will be clear. There will not be anything to hinder you. I am not saying that everything will go smoothly for you. However, I can give you ten instances to try what I am telling you about. When a great misfortune comes on you, which you cannot solve, say to yourself, "Let me try this Lord." Say, "Let's see what that Master tells us about his Lord, let's pray to his Lord to see whether He will help us." Call upon my Lord. When you cannot solve a certain issue, leave it to my Lord, let Him solve it. If in these ten cases, it does not happen as I say, I will give you ten more attempts to know my Lord. Then if you do not come to know Him, I will give you ten more attempts. If you then do not succeed, call me. On the 30th time I will come and when I come everything will happen. Until then I will leave you free. There is one positive science, that must create the future culture, the future high character qualities of the mothers, of the fathers, of the brothers and of the sisters. That is the new culture that must be built. It will be built in the face of one society in which evil will be loved without being made and the good will be loved by being made. Hatred will be loved, without us doing it. Love will be loved by us by making it. The only one powerful thing in the world is Love, which uplifts life. Believe in Love. Love, this is God, who shows benevolence to all, Who has a relation to your mothers and fathers, to the priests, to the teachers, to the statesmen, to the servants, to the cattle, to every living thing. Love this Lord. You say, we have to be happy. In the future, not only the people, but our cattle, hens and all animals must know, that we love God. They must feel our happiness, to understand that in us has occurred one inner social transformation. All beings must know that. "Be like the children!" Believe in your Father and do not attribute to Him your weaknesses. Do not say, "This Lord will be dealing with me." The greatness of this Lord, about Whom I am talking to you, is recognized by this, He deals with the smallest things, with which no one else in the world deals with.

5, p. 598

I call learned people those who understand the laws of life and the laws of nature. Life does not lie in the many things we wish for ourselves. Life is in the little, in the microscopic. You can be a wealthy man and not be able to use your wealth. You can have a granary full of wheat and still die from hunger. You can have only one loaf of bread in your bag and still be alive. It is up to man to process the little. The little, but processed, is worth more, than the much, which is never processed.

5, p. 601

    Everyone aspires towards the great in the world and ignore the little. We can say that all sufferings and misfortunes in the world come from that greed for the great, for the unknown, for such things, which even after we have them, we still cannot keep them. You can become a king so you can conquer the whole Earth, but tomorrow you grow old, others come, dethrone you, replace you and at the end, you die.

5, p. 601

    In the word "love," I understand, something clear which the children understand. He who loves me, he is ready for me to do anything that I love. This is what Love means. He who does not love me, he is not ready to do anything that I want. This is the simplest explanation of the meaning of the word love.

5, p. 602

    You want to know why the Lord has created you. Do not ask anything about that. All of you are touching this issue. Do not touch it. Why your Father has created you, do not ask. Why does He love you, do not ask this question. What do you understand from this, that your father loves you? Somebody can love you for the only reason that he can take something from you. You love somebody. Why do you love him? There are two reasons for which you love a man: because you either want to take something from him; or because you want to give him something. Sometimes, I consider Love as one big burden which a man carries. So, oftentimes this load is too heavy for him and he cannot carry it. That's why he is looking for an opportunity to unload himself. When he finds somebody, he starts to love him, he unloads himself and gives the other person half of his load. Then he says, "Glory to God, that I found one man to whom I can unload myself." Thus, he is grateful that he has started to love somebody. That is how I look at the issue from a purely childish viewpoint. When somebody starts to love me, I say, yes, this man wants to put half of his load on my back, but this man will see whether I can carry it or not. If I can carry it, he will unload himself completely. If I cannot carry it, it is better that he does not unload himself, because I will leave him with half of his load in the middle of the road. I often hear somebody tell another one, I do not want his Love. Yes, he does not want his love, because it is heavy, he cannot carry it. That kind of love is heavy.

Now I want you to read between the lines. What I am saying now, is not yet essential.

5, p. 604

When somebody loves you, do not ask whether he loves you. When you love somebody, do not tell him why you love him. If you try to explain the Love, you will make a crack, you will tear that chain in which Love moves. From the creation of the world till now, I have been looking at this issue. Everyone who has attempted to know who and how he loves him, he has always lost the Love.

5, p. 605

When it is said in the Scripture, to love your neighbor, this is a law for extending one's life. When you are loved and when you love, your life will be extended. Why do you have to love? So your life is continues. Why do we have to love God? So our life is ceaseless. Why do we have to love our neighbor? So our life is ceaseless. These are the two important laws in the world. This is a philosophy, that has meaning. Somebody asks, can we go without Love? It can be without Love, but that is limited love. If you want to have the idea to love God and to love your neighbor, this is already a different issue. The issue lies in this, that we have to be ready to love.

5, p. 606

Today all are asking what the causes are for the world's sufferings. The sufferings have two origins: either from too much Love; or from Lovelessness. Man can suffer for the only reason, that they do not love him, but he can suffer and from this, that they love him a lot. The mother loves her child so much that she does not let the child go anywhere. Wherever the child goes, she always follows the child. Sometimes no one loves you, no one takes care of you, then you are suffering. Thus lies the issue with the sufferings in my mind. There are two reasons for the sufferings: either they love you a lot; or they do not love you at all.

5, p. 606

The beauty in life lies in this: you love. When you find somebody, who loves you, your mind begins to work. When you love somebody, your mind again works, but there is a difference in both cases. All learned people, who study science; all religious people, who are dealing with religion; all politicians, who deal with politics; have in their foundation two situations. Man works, so they love him, this is one situation; man works, so as to love, this is the other situation. The first law is the source of life. There lies man's power. If man comes out from that situation, he will have one positive science.

5, p. 608

It is an easy thing for a man to be happy. But how? You cannot be happy if you are not loved. You cannot be happy if you do not love. You can say that you do not want to know about people. This is true, but nevertheless you still have to have at least one to love, One definitely you must love. If you love neither God, nor your neighbor, then whom are you going to love? Then what will be the meaning of your life?

5, p. 608

Somebody wants to become rich and thinks that when he becomes rich, he will become happy. It is so, but only for the reasonable one. If a man is smart, he can become happy, but if he is not smart, he cannot become happy. I want to be strong but in order to be strong, you must first be smart. If you are smart and strong, you will know how to use your strength. I want to be a learned person, but you must be reasonable also, because you will know how to use your knowledge. If you are not smart, with that knowledge you will create for yourself the greatest misfortunes.

5, p. 608

You shall connect every day with living nature. When you get connected with it, you will rejuvenate yourself. This must be constantly happening. In nature there is no stagnation. She rejuvenates things, and every day she brings something new, something alive. She never leaves the man with the old. It deposits in man something new over and over throughout the whole day. He, who understands that and can make use of it, is good; he, who cannot understand it and does make use of it, is good, too.

5, p. 609

You want to find a man to love you. This is natural, because he who loves you, prolongs your life with his Love. In general, Love prolongs life. Christ says: "I came to give life to people and give it over-abundantly." *(John 10: 10)* Since Christ loves the people, that is why He gave them life. He says: "The thief does not come, except to steal, to destroy and to kill. I came to give them live in abundance." Now you shall apply this law in your psychic law, so you know what is possible. Every thought, which brings in life, is the Christ principle. I came to give them life. Every thought, which takes the life from you, that thought is not Divine, it is the second situation, it is the thief, who comes to steal and to destroy. Every wish, that brings life, this is the first principle. Every wish, that takes out life, is the second principle. When somebody does not love you, do not ask why he does not love you. The issue is solved. You do not need this man to love you. What need do you have for the devil to love you? What need does the sheep have of your love? If you love her, you will eat her. There are people, whose love you must have no need for. When one of these people do not love you, it is a bigger happiness for you, than if he loves you. This is how you should be thinking. Sometimes you are disappointed with yourself, that you have not achieved what you had in mind. You are deluding yourself. Be grateful/Say thank you/, that you have not achieved what you have wished for. You are not the first factor in the world. The first factor in the world is God, Who has created everything and Who has drawn the plan. He has drawn a certain plan, which is gradually being realized. In the second place, as a second factor in life, is your soul. If you work in accordance with the law of God, you will be happy. You can be happy this very day, but you can be happy in a year or in ten years, or in a hundred years, in a thousand, in 10,000 years and so on. There are things which can be achieved this very day. For example, this very day you can learn to sing. I define a term of ten years for one to become a doctor, for he, who wants to become a doctor. For a paint artist I also define ten years, for him to become a musician. More than ten years are not needed. From one to ten years is enough for the achievement of something. Ten years work is enough for the success of human life. He who does not understand the digits from one to ten, he will not have success.

5, p. 610

In which digit is the woman in? Do you know that? It is said, that in the sixth day God made man. In what day then did He make the woman? Did He do this before noon or did He make her in the afternoon? Adam was the last creation of the Lord, but then He pulled out a rib from him and from it He made woman. So man remained as a creation before the last one of the Lord, but the woman the last one. Therefore, and up to this day the woman solves everything. In other words, the feelings are the last thing which we can try. If you think that behind Love you can find another thing, you do not understand anything. Love is the last border. What is there behind Love? There is something scary. Whoever has gone beyond Love, got his hair gray. He repents and returns back. "At tomorrow's day." In tomorrow's day are hidden all opportunities. As I see you, you all want to be happy. Some of you want to be musicians, paint artists, rich traders, others want to be beautiful, you want to be just about anything. That's why you all pray to the Lord to achieve these wishes of yours. You pray, but in the end you do not achieve anything. With this I do not want to judge you. You are acting very right, but you are not smart. I will tell you what I mean that you are not smart. Imagine that you have one good professor in music and you go to ask him every day to teach you to play some musical instrument, but you study nothing. You only ask him to teach you how to play, but you do not study anything. When he gives you a lesson, you have to play the instrument, you have to exercise. I say, I have prayed for a full 20 years to the Lord, but have not received anything. Why? You have prayed, but you have not worked at anything. No, work is required in the world.

5, p. 611

If one bad wish has entered you and you pity it and you do not put it in its place, it will defeat you.

5, p. 612

Each wish, which cannot bring you something good is not for you. There are many wishes which are not for you. From here I pull the following law, always, when two virtues come one after the other, they produce one mishap. Never allow two virtues to happen to you one after the other. This looks to you a bit contradictory, but I will explain the law in the following way. A friend of yours has treated you with a very good meal. You just fed yourself up, another friend of yours comes and invites you also for a nice meal. In this case, refuse the second lunch, postpone it for another day. Do not over-sate yourself with unnecessary wishes.

5, p. 613

I often talk about the genius. What are the distinguishing traits of the genius? In the word genius I understand one, who is not confused even when he is in the greatest difficulties. He is in the condition to get out from the most difficult situation, in which he is put. The genius is like an acrobat, wherever you lock him up, he will still get out. The saint, too, not only does he understand things, but he can get out from any difficulty. The saint, in these conditions, moulds and from the ordinary things creates an art work. In order to create, you must be a saint, but in order to defeat the difficulties, you must be a genius. If you do not have in yourself any genius, you cannot defeat even the smallest difficulty. In order to be able to create something, you must have the mind of a saint. In a given instance you can have the mind of a saint. Consequently, at least in one moment, you can be a saint and in the next moment you can be a genius. If you know how to get out from your difficulties, in which you have gotten yourself into, you are a genius. If you know how to pass on the knowledge you have, you are a saint. If you cannot pass on your knowledge to another one, you are not a saint. Then I look at the genius and the sainthood for myself. **The genius in the world is known by this, that the geniuses can solve the difficulties.** There are family, social, religious, political, national, individual and many more difficulties. For this purpose genius people are required, who can pull out humanity from these difficulties. For these, more than one genius must come into the world. Many must come, I ask, in this situation, in which you are in, what can you do? You have a wealth of experience, but you do not have the opportunity to find out when you will be a genius. Sometimes you feel nervous or upset, you think that nothing will come out of you. This is the best condition for you. For the present day scientists it is said that they are missing something. It is not like that. The genius, too, is put in the worse conditions to work and cope with the difficulties of life. The first thing that happens is that he begins to dream and then he finds the right way.

Therefore, the occult disciple must see the genius in his understandings. The genius man must not hesitate in his virtues and must always say, everything works for good. When the genius man, takes one piece of charcoal, he transforms it into a diamond. When the genius takes one apple seed, he puts it into the ground, so it can grow up. When the genius enters among the bad people, they become good, because he knows how to work among them in his way.

This often happens, when somebody is told that what he wants to achieve is impossible, he gets discouraged and stops in his path for his wish. This man is telling you, that this thing what you are seeking, you cannot find. He is telling you the Truth. This man is telling you, that the way along the path which you are walking, is not a good one, there is another one, which you must take and in which you will achieve your wishes. The wishes are not achieved in one way only or in one course of action. There are many ways and many courses of actions through which the wishes can be achieved, but each man must find the one, the only way, that only one method, which is specific for his wishes. Somebody thinks, that there is only one way for all. No, for each man there is a specific way, a specific method for him to achieve his wishes and for the realization of his thoughts. Consequently, everyone must find his specific way, through which you can achieve your genius.

5, p. 615

If you study Love, as I study it, you will find the meaning of life. Then there will be understanding among the people. When you meet one man, you shall see in him firstly his good side. The issue is not when you see one man, to want only him to help you, but you both mutually shall help each other. When two people love each other, the first thing that is required from them is that there must be a mutual exchange between them. In this lies the meaning of life. Do not just ask that only you are to be loved. Life lies in this, to love and be loved. This is the tomorrow's day, this is the today's day. Today is a Divine day.

5, p. 618

Now many talk about the other world, but if I describe it, I will describe it as such, what they cannot imagine. If people describe it, they will describe it, like the way this world is, the Earthly world, but they will describe wrongfully. In the other world there are things, which they, in no way, can comprehend. There is something particularly beautiful there. When you meet a soul in the other world, when it looks at you, you will see something beautiful in its look, something specific, full with Love. Whatever benefits you have, this soul will be glad, as if it was the soul who was acquiring them. There, there is competition, like it is on Earth among the people. There, in the other world, each one is glad with the acquisitions of the others. This law is still not learned on Earth.

So be glad for all that, which God has prepared for you. Be glad for all that, which God has put in your ears. Be glad of the sufferings, with which God has honored you, because He has put in them something good for you alone. Be glad for all of your virtues, for all of your opportunities! Be glad for everything! This is the Word of God.

5, p. 615

In nature there are two moments of studying. The first moment is of the Providence, when God works upon us. This people accept in one way or another, and define it differently. The other moment is when man himself works on himself and makes efforts to add something to the work of God.

5, p. 620

If you acquire knowledge, this teaching will be for you, not for the others. You want the world to be good and the people to be good. If one man is good, he will be good for himself, but not for you. You do not trust in the good of others, but rely in the Good which is inside you. This is the understanding, in the progress of man. If a man alone is not good, this is a result of his studying. You cannot be good if you have not studied. Somebody wants to do good, but how will he do it? You are a tailor and you want to pattern draw one garment. In order to pattern draw it as needed, you must have studied, to know how to pattern draw it. If you pattern draw it properly, you will uplift yourself. If you do not pattern draw it properly, you will lose, you will ruin the garment.

I say, in the contemporary Christian world there is a danger that people think they can go without studying. They think they can pass or move up without studying. The ox can pass without studying, but he knows it for himself. Who would like to go through the life of the ox? The fish goes without studying as well, but who from you would like to be a fish? I can tell you about many beings which go without studying. I can tell you about many beings, which do not have any aspirations, which for thousands of years only eat and drink, which have no science, no religion, no faith, no idea about God, they are not interested in anything. The clams are not interested in anything, they are closed in their shells.

5, p. 621

You are talking now about the social situation, the hereditary traits. Heredity was created by you. It does not play a big role. It plays a role, but it is not a powerful factor in the world. In the world there are two powerful factors, which play an important role. These are the human heart or the human feelings and the human mind or the human thoughts. There are no more important factors than these. To them correspond Love and Divine Wisdom. These are powerful forces, which transform and push the world towards progress. On the basis of that, we go from the lower to the higher.

5, p. 629

That religion, which does not awaken in man the higher abilities for understanding and distinguishing, is not a true religion. When the higher abilities in man are awakened, he comes to the situation of being the master of himself.

5, p. 630

We have to study those currents which happen in our heart, in our mind, in our brain and to make fine distinctions between them, to watch how these currents influence the common physical and psychic life of man. Our consciousness must be awakened. When a bad thought enters your mind, you have to find out its origins. When a bad feeling comes in you, again you have to find its origins, to know where it came from. If a man does not know from where the bad thoughts and feelings come, he can often become a slave or a victim of these bad feelings and thoughts in himself.

5, p. 630

Imagine, that somebody has sympathy for you and you are connected with him. At one point, in him arises the desire to steal. After some time you receive this desire of his through your internal radio. If you do not know, that this desire comes from your acquaintance, you will think that it is yours, and you will wonder where the desire to steal came from? You are not the cause for that thought. What shall you do? Since you are in connection with him by means of sympathy, then you shall send him a counter thought, that this which he is doing is not good. This what he is doing, is not nice, it is not good to steal. Despite that it is not nice to steal, he must put something in his safe. This is the way through which you can help all of your close ones, in whom arise bad thoughts and desires. So, to every negative or bad thought put one good counter thought.

5, p. 631

Many fathers are sick only because their children do not lead a good life. Many mothers are sick, because their sons do not live well. He with whomever he is connected, bears the consequences of his life. If you are connected with a man who does not live well, you can pay with your life. You have to understand this law. If your son does not live well, you shall tell him, "Son, because I am connected with you, your bad life reflects on me, too. I have given you birth, I have become a guarantor for you and that is why I want you to live well. Look to straighten out your life, not to bring my old age prematurely to the grave."

By living her bad life, the daughter can ruin the life of her mother, but the son with his bad life can ruin the life of his father.

5, p. 632

If your love for your friend brings life in him, it is right; if it does not bring life in your friend, it is not right, it is not in its place.

I say, all people, who walk upon the way in the new teaching, they must have the brightest views, scientific views based on data.

5, p. 632

Whoever has true knowledge in himself, you will recognize from his, that from his brain comes out one specific light with a specific color, which is a very pleasant color. He who has a big light in himself, he possesses great self-confidence. He is like a master paint-artist, who understands his art, whose brush moves correctly. He who does not understand his art, his brush does not go correctly.

5, p. 633

There is a prayer, which in certain cases can be read in Bulgarian or in English or in Sanskrit or in Greek. Why? They are stronger in that case. There are prayers, which in Bulgarian are the strongest. The same can be said for specific words and for specific sentences. There are instances, when in the Bulgarian language some words are exactly put in their own place, then they have power. When it is like that, they cannot be replaced with words from any other language.

5, p. 633

In the world there are two laws. Towards God and towards a neighbor. If I do not fulfill my word given to God and I do not fulfill my word given to my neighbor, I ask then, where is the man?

Now let's come to a common situation. There are instances in a man's life, when he comes to some principles which he must test, he sees that if he decides to speak the truth, he must depart from this world. In such cases he must prefer to depart from this world, than to give up certain principles, than to deny the truth. That is what happened with Christ. He said: "I came into the world to testify for the truth," *(John 18: 37)* but because there are no conditions for this, I prefer to depart from this world, than to deny the truth and remain on Earth." Christ possessed the power to free Himself, but He did not use His power to defend Himself. In the Gospel it is said, that when the Roman soldiers came to Him, He asked them: "Who are you looking for?" "If you are seeking me, here am I, but leave the others." He freed His disciples. Christ did not use his power for his redemption. If He had used His power, to keep His Earthly life, He would have lost His heavenly life. He preferred to lose His Earthly life, but to acquire the heavenly. He preferred death to say the Truth, than to keep silent before the truth.

5, p. 634

I say, those who depart for the other world, enter into us and begin to live together with us. In this way they become one with us and we one with them. Therefore, I say, in one body can live not only one soul, but thousands of souls and all can live together. To you it may seem strange when I say, that in one body can live thousands of souls. I ask, how many people can live in a hotel? Can, in an army barrack, live only one soldier? No, thousands of soldiers live in an army barrack. *Man is one big building, in which thousands of people can enter and live together.* The more that reasonable beings enter to live in you, the better for you. When we say, that we are reasonable beings, we understand, that we are connected with all reasonable beings on Earth. We are at the same time connected and with all reasonable beings who live in heaven. Consequently, we have in our disposition, heaven, with all of its archives, with all of its knowledge. This is what we call inspiration. A poet sits down to write. One reasonable being from the invisible world comes and starts to dictate by telling him what to write. The poet writes, but the reasonable being is dictating to him. The poet becomes inspired and writes. Some people, who deal with spiritualism, write on paper, but nothing comes out of it. Then they will say, that the spirit told him something and he wrote it down. Nothing has told him the spirit. When the spirit talks, he talks clearly and definitively. When the Divine Spirit comes in man, whatever it promises, happens. If He promises you to become a king, you will become a king. You are ill, the Divine Spirit comes into you and tells you: "Tomorrow you will be healthy." You become healthy. You have an exam to take. The Spirit comes in you and tells you: "You will pass well your exam." Truly you pass the exam well. You are a pregnant woman. The Spirit comes and tells you: "You will give a birth well." Whatever He has said, thus it happens. You are a slave somewhere. The Spirit comes and tells you: "Tomorrow you will be free." Truly, the next day you are already free. You are at sea and a great catastrophe is unfolding. The Spirit says: "Do not worry, everything will calm down. "Truly, soon, everything calms down. So, wherever the Divine Spirit is, there things happen in accordance of how He has determined. A man and a woman get in a quarrel. Now they will be calling a third person to help them to reconcile. They should not be calling a man from outside to reconcile them. Let them call the Lord Who is in them so He can reconcile them. The woman must say, Lord, You, Who are in me and in my beloved, in my neighbor, come to our help so we can understand each other. When two beloved cannot come to an understanding with each other, they do not love each other. You say, once upon a time we have loved each other, but now we do not. You are lying to yourself. Do not make up illusions for yourself and believe in them, do not self deceive yourself. **Love never changes**.

5, p. 635

Man carries in himself, this with which he is born. The smart one, who is born smart, always remains such. The fool, who is born foolish, will always remain foolish. Do not think that this is by accident. With this I only want to confirm one truth. This, what is put in man, no one can take away from him.

5, p. 636

Now you want to be strong. You have a little bread with you. Through faith this bread can be increased. If you have faith and you know how to take out the energy from the wheat grain, there will be so much energy in one loaf of bread, which if you can take it out, you will be able to feed yourself for at least 6 months.

5, p. 646

It is said in the Scripture, that God lives in heaven, but He lives in the hearts of the humble, too. If God lives wholly in your heart, then what will you need? The day on which God comes to live in your heart, all of your things will be set right. Do not seek to be set right materially. Your daughter and son must have the same enlightenment, as you have. If your husband cannot love God, as you love Him and if your daughters and sons do not love God, as you love Him, you cannot ask for blessings for them.

5, p. 647

So, we have to separate the essentials in life from that which is not essential and on those essentials we have to always rely on. The ordinary ideas, which the contemporary people have for social order, for mothers and fathers, for brothers and sisters, they do not correspond to that reality, upon which is created the brotherhood. A true brother is only he, who is one with you in spirit and in soul and in mind and in heart. True sisters and friends are only those, who are one with you and in mind and in heart and in spirit and in soul. They must share your fate in all conditions, not only by interest. They must equally share the things and to equally help each other. The help lies in the human thoughts, but not in the human feelings. It is not the words which man says, but his deeds that are important. A deed must be done on time.

5, p. 647

Until man comes to the situation to put his trust in Love, he is not in the right way. When he begins to trust in Love, he is now in the right way. Consequently, the truth excludes from itself all delusions, but includes all virtues. What is the Truth? This, which in a given case, excludes from man all delusions, all evil deeds, all injustices, all evil, everything bad, but includes in it all good, all sublime, that is the Truth. Whatever in a given case brings into a man's life meaning, whatever ennobles, that is the Truth. This, which can take me out from one condition and puts me into another, that is Truth; this, what has always uplifted me and in the future will uplift me, that is Truth. No matter how I define the Truth, I still cannot define it. The Truth has practical meaning in its application. Now a question will come up, can we apply that? We can; there is a line of rules for that. They are not extreme rules. Before all, man's strength is constantly in development, it is not something that can be achieved at once and then stop. When the children enter first grade, they do not study everything at once.

5, p. 648

This, which satisfies the soul is Love. This which satisfies the spirit is Wisdom. This which gives meaning to everything is the Truth. Path without ruin, truth without doubt and life without suffering - this is immortality. Youth is the garment of life. Light is the garment of knowledge. Freedom is the garment of health. Life without virtues is a garden without flowers, is trees without fruits. Do not seek this, which you do not need. Do not carry within yourself items which do not satisfy you. Be always free and never harness yourself. Put the harness to rest, but your strength to work. Put fear as a servant to reason. Put charity as a helper of your heart.

"Blessed is he, who eats bread in the Kingdom of God." *(Luke 14: 15)*

The living bread in the world, that is the Divine, in which we every day feed ourselves. This bread is the conductor of life. For this to be understood is required a better understanding.

5, p. 650

Reasonableness in the world goes by a completely different law. It means to be able to overcome all difficulties which exist within yourself. Present day people have thousands of cases, where they can test their faith and reasonableness. Have you ever tried to check your faith? When your hair turns white, can you blacken it? Why are you disturbed with the white hair and you desire black? The white always gives more, but the black takes more. The black decoration, these are the economist people, but the white color, these are the generous people, the philanthropists. The capital of those people goes out. Therefore when a man grows old, he spends everything.

5, p. 650

You are seeing that my hair turned white, but now I am studying the law of generosity. To keep giving. However, I never give away meaninglessly, I study generosity and give away according to all rules. When somebody comes to me and wants me to do something good, I'll review all of his bills from the past. When I do for him one microscopic good, I'll take ten signatures on a promissory note. You will say that this is stinginess. Put aside your understandings. Love is extremely generous and extremely demanding.

5, p. 652

It is a law, no one can love you, until you give them something from yourself. The children love their mother, because she has given them something from herself. We all love God, because, He has given a lot of things from Himself. We have to love God, because, everything that we have, is given to us by Him. If we do not love Him, we put ourselves on a crooked foundation, on a dangerous way. You say, that you believe in God. You must believe in God, in Love, because from faith, which you have, from this Love depends not only your happiness, but that of your wife, your children and the whole of your family as well. It all depends on your faith.

"Blessed is he, who eats from the living bread, from the bread, that is in God's Kingdom." *(John 6: 51)* When you eat this bread, you must know that in it is God's power. Everything that happens in the world, has a certain solution, and that solution is determined by the bread which you eat.

5, p. 654

    The old order can no longer be tolerated. All people require something new. The new teaching, the Christ teaching lies in the following law: "Where there are two or three gathered in My name, there am I among them." *(Matthew 18: 20)* Since the man and the woman, these are parts of the whole man. The man is one half and the woman the other half. Consequently, the man and the woman, gathered together, this is the man, but between them is God.

5, p. 654

    Then some ask, "Why do people get divorced?" For their lovelessness. The man and the woman must be rich by mind and by heart. They must not be weak. All people must be healthy. The sick people must not marry; the foolish people must not marry; the heartless people must not marry. Man, who enters the Divine way, must be without infirmities.

5, p. 655

    The material life is needed for man, as the clay is needed by the pottery maker. When he is working that mud, he still will get dirty, but when he makes it into a dough and bake from it some pottery, the pottery maker will still take a few coins for food for his children. If that clay didn't exist, what would that pottery maker have made? When you work with that mud, your hands will still become rough, you still will dirty them or they will lose their softness, but that is another issue. Without this mud in the material world it cannot be. There are certain things, which are necessary with the contemporary development of man. This idea must lie in your minds. There are no bad things in the world. In essence there are bad things only when we do not understand what is given to us, and we cannot make use of it.

It is said: "At the beginning was the Word." *(John 1:1)* Everything happens through It. However, we the people on Earth, have new ideas, we want to put these ideas in our life with the goal to improve it. We can do that. Truly, if our new ideas, which we put in our life, are not in the condition to improve our lives, we have to change them. For surely if it is not like that, we have to abandon these ideas of ours. Keep only that idea, only that feeling and only that action in you, which in a given case helps to create in you one urge, one impulse, to be elevated.

5, p. 663

I say, man cannot free himself from a bad habit of his, from one mistake of his, from one crime of his and from one deed of his, until he first changes his thoughts. You cannot change one habit of yours and free yourself from it and as well from your mistake and crimes, until you change your feelings and your actions. A sick man came to me and I told him, "You can easily heal yourself." "How will I heal myself?" "When you imagine that you are healthy." "How will I imagine, that I am healthy, when I am sick?" "There namely lies your evil. Then namely you cannot be healing yourself. This is going around in circles." A poor man came to me and said, "Do you know how much I am in deep water? All of my things do not go well." "Imagine, that you are rich." "How will I imagine that I am rich when I have no money in my pocket? If I have something in my pocket, I can imagine." "In this situation how can I imagine, that I am rich? That is why namely, you cannot fix your things right. In this lies the reality." That farmer, who sows the wheat in his field, he must believe, that in the following year he will have more wheat to reap. When he puts the wheat in the field, it will transform in such a way, that the next year from 10 kg. he will collect 100. The farmer knows how to transform the wheat. When a sick person comes to you, whom you must cure, you must sow in him one simple truth, that he will recover to good health. When he accepts this truth in himself, like one seed, it will grow up and produce a fruit. When you see in yourself the thought, that you are healthy, you truly will be healthy.

5, p. 664

Let's assume that you are a religious man. In the morning when you get up, you have to use at least 15 minutes for reasoning. 15 minutes you are obliged to stop and wait, because each 15 minutes from the invisible world there is one train. You, when you wake up, this time of 15 minutes, you shall not use for anything else, you shall pray. If you do not pray properly as you are supposed to, on that day the greatest mishaps will come on your head.

5, p. 677

We say, that we have Love for God. The time for you to die has come near. Say, Lord, from dead people you have no need. Let me live to work for You, to live on Earth to work, to love You. We, the contemporary people, must learn to love the Lord. All the mishaps emerge from that fact, that we do not love the Lord.

5, p. 684

If all of us are on the right track, if our beliefs from thousands of years ago are not delusions, let them give a result. In my view, one creed, which has a result, that creed is the right one. That creed, the Love for God, when we make a connection among all people, to live well, to love each other, to help each other, that creed is the creed in the world. Regardless of what the nations are, let them be Bulgarians, English and these nations are to mutually help each other. The relation, that one is a father, a mother or a son or a daughter, between teachers and students, there must be an exchange amongst them. This relationship must work, between them there shall be a connection of Love, when everyone enjoys the situation.

5, p. 684

Somebody came and has insulted you. Make an experiment and say, I am giving you one thousand leva (BG currency) for this word, if you tell me a second time an insulting word, I will give you more. How many of you would have given a thousand leva for one insulting word? It is a new philosophy of life. It is when Christ preached: "Love thy enemies." To love your enemy, to give him a thousand leva each time. This man is doing you harm, but you love him! To love him, because in this man there is a Divine beginning. If you treat the Divine beginning, properly and as you should, then God, when He awakens in him, will pay you ten times for that favor, which you have done for him. You, when you love the bad man, do not love him for his badness, but because of Him, Who lives in him. You will be loved not for your own sake. We are loved, not because of our own sake, we are loved for the Divine in us. It is love. For as much as a man manifests the Divine, from there emerges Love. Without the Divine in the world, there can be no Love, there can be no happiness, man's heart cannot progress, a man cannot be young. He will always be old, discontent in life.

5, p. 685

A young man is he, who is ready to do a favor to all. A young man is he, who bears all the sufferings, who bears all the hardships. A young man is he, who studies, who loves, who does not lie, who is not afraid. He is fearless. A young man is he who works and pays on time everything. A young man is he who is upright, he who is not upright, he is an old man. A young man, in my view, is the man upright in all of his situations. A young man can be anyone, if he only knows the means.

Christ says to Peter: "When you were young, you were going wherever you wanted, when you get old, you will go where you do not want to." *(John 21: 18)* Christ tells him: "Look that you do not get old!" Whereas if you get old, the only thing that is left for you, is the burial. Therefore, I am telling you, be young, be ready to serve Love.

5, p. 687

Life on Earth has only one meaning: to know God.

Book, ***The Wellspring of Good***

BIBLIOGRAPHY:

1. The Tuning/Harmonization of the Human Soul, Vol. 3, Sofia, 2009
2. The Two Divine Visits (1941/42)
3. The Hero Path (Sunday Lectures, Selected)
4. Savaat Amon Ra (Sunday Lectures, 1926)
5. This Is the Living Bread (Sunday Lectures, 23.09.1934-15.09.35)
(I am not sure if the above books are translated into English as of now.)

If you want to progress, do the will of God and not yours.

A man's true progress is defined by his Love for all people and for all living beings.

The only way to God is Love. Only he who loves can find God.

Love God in all people! In Love lies the solution of all issues.

CPSIA information can be obtained
at www.ICGtesting.com
Printed in the USA
LVHW091950111019
633944LV00001B/73/P